I'm So Happy You're Here

ALSO BY LIZ CLIMO

You're Dad

You're Mom

Best Bear Ever!

Rory the Dinosaur: Me and My Dad

Rory the Dinosaur Wants a Pet

Rory the Dinosaur Needs a Christmas Tree

The Little World of Liz Climo

Lobster Is the Best Medicine

I'm So Happy You're Here

a little book about why you're great.

by liz climo

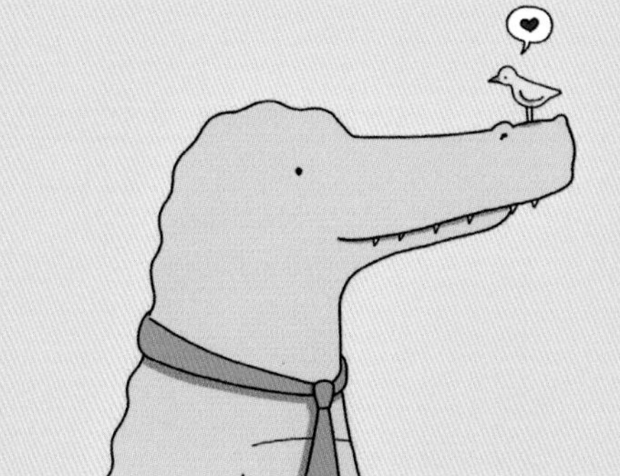

FLATIRON
BOOKS
NEW YORK

Printed in China. For information, address Flatiron Books, 120 Broadway, New York, NY 10271.

www.flatironbooks.com

The Library of Congress Cataloging-in-Publication Data is available upon request.

ISBN 978-1-250-84144-5 (paper over board)
ISBN 978-1-250-84145-2 (ebook)

Our books may be purchased in bulk for promotional, educational, or business use. Please contact your local bookseller or the Macmillan Corporate and Premium Sales Department at 1-800-221-7945, extension 5442, or by email at MacmillanSpecialMarkets@macmillan.com.

First Edition: 2022

10 9 8 7 6 5 4 3 2 1

FOR YOU

HOORAY!
It's YOU!

I was *hoping* I'd see . . .

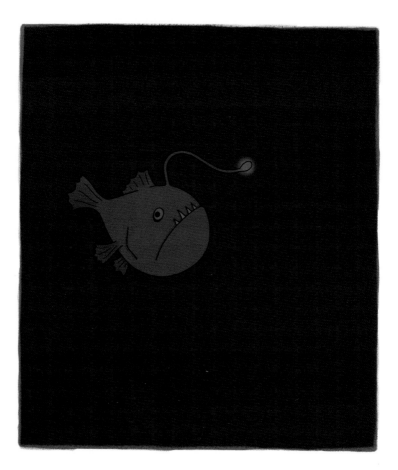

your warm, smiling face looking back at me.

I'm so happy you're here.

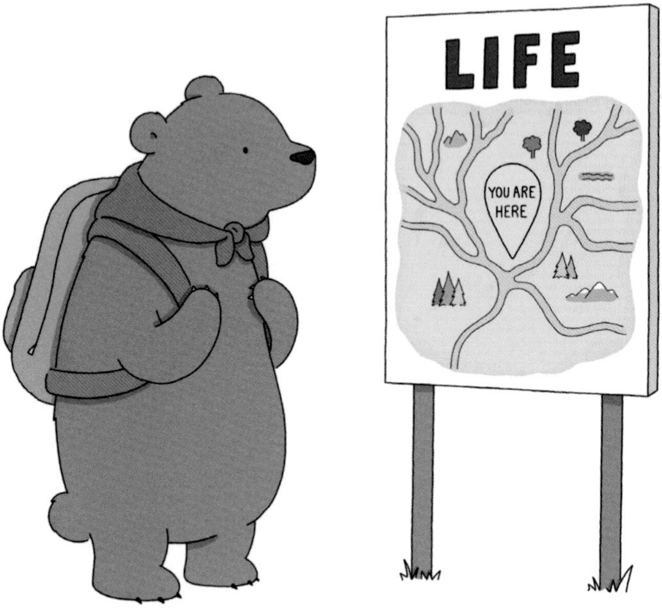

LIFE
YOU ARE HERE

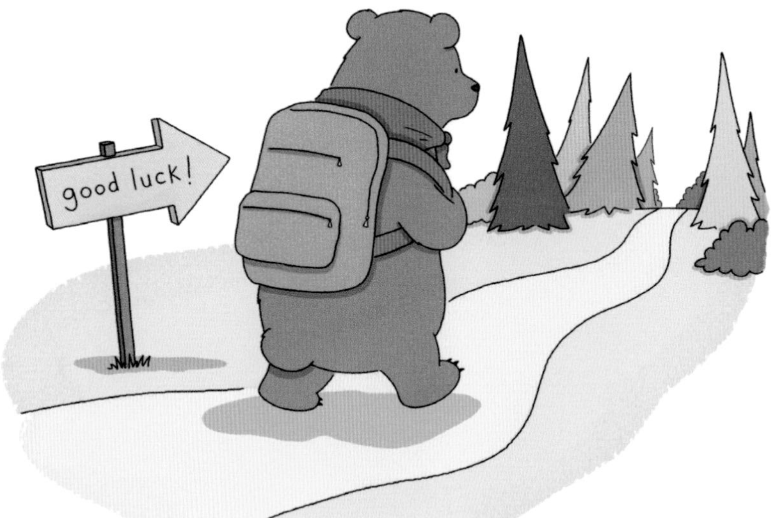
good luck!

That you've picked up this book.

What, don't believe me?

come on!

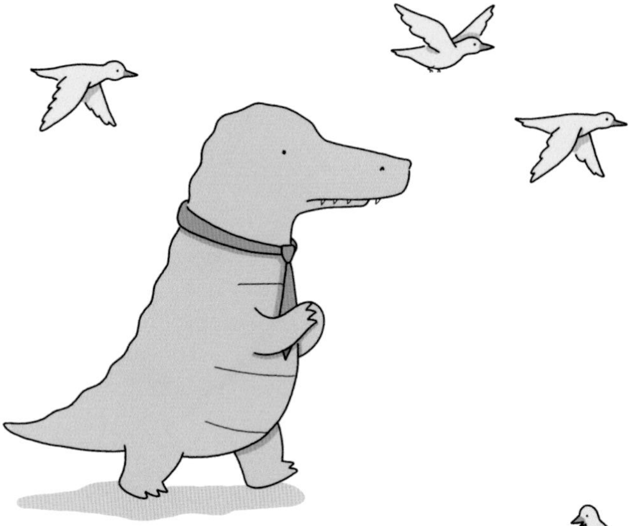

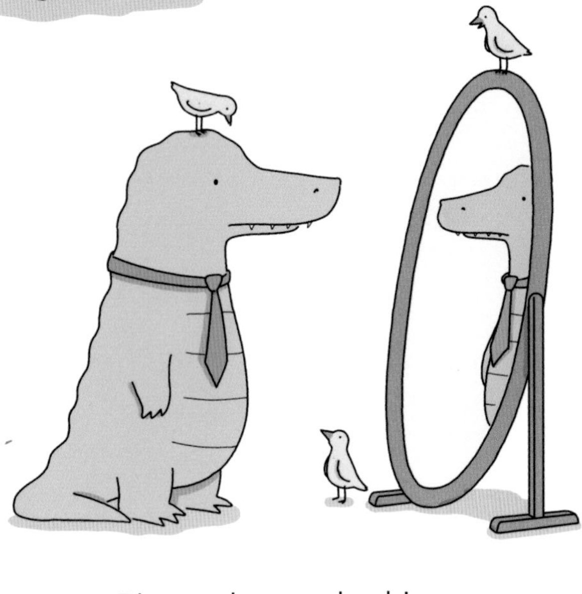

Please, have a look!

You're the only one like you,
and let me be clear:

The world is much better
because you are here.

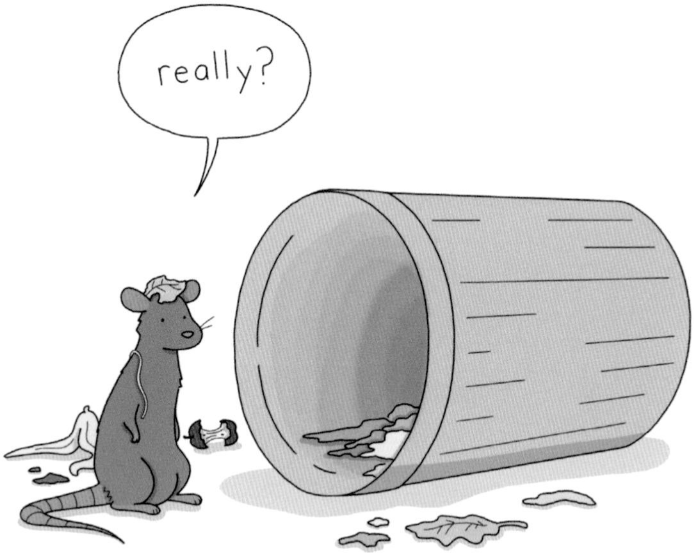
really?

Trust me on this.

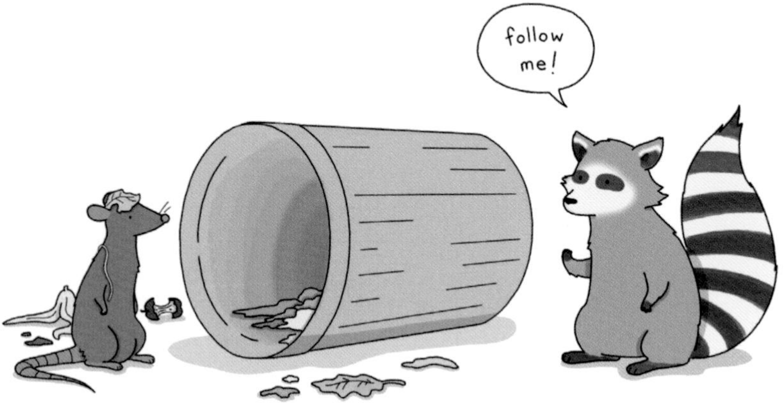
follow me!

I’ve asked all the rest.

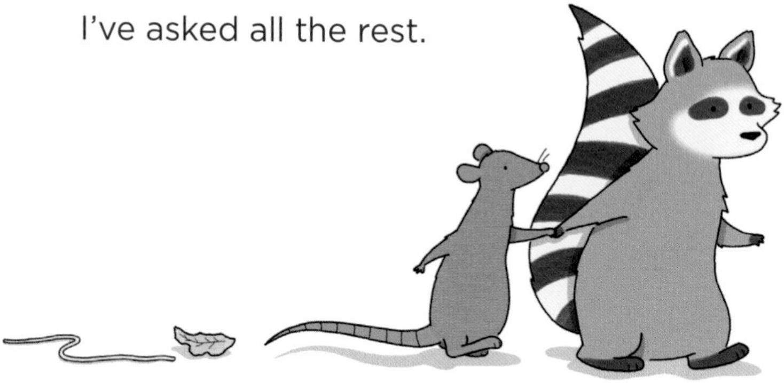

The results are unanimous:

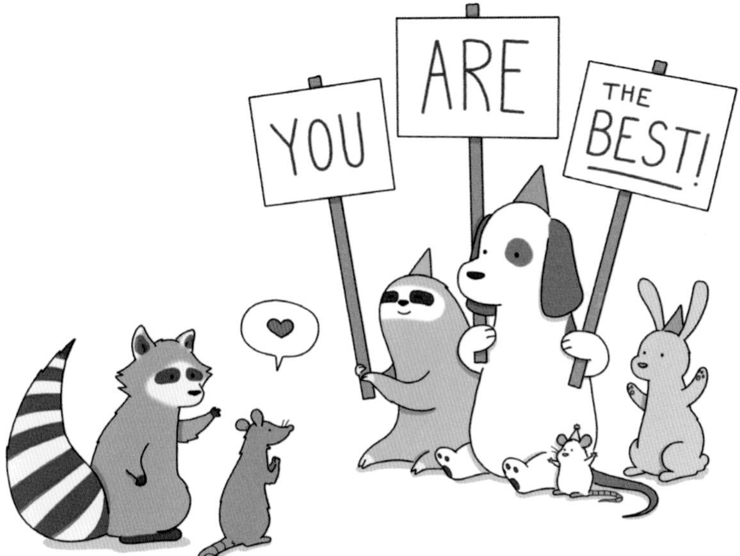
YOU
ARE
THE
BEST!

Don't ever let anyone
say it's not true.

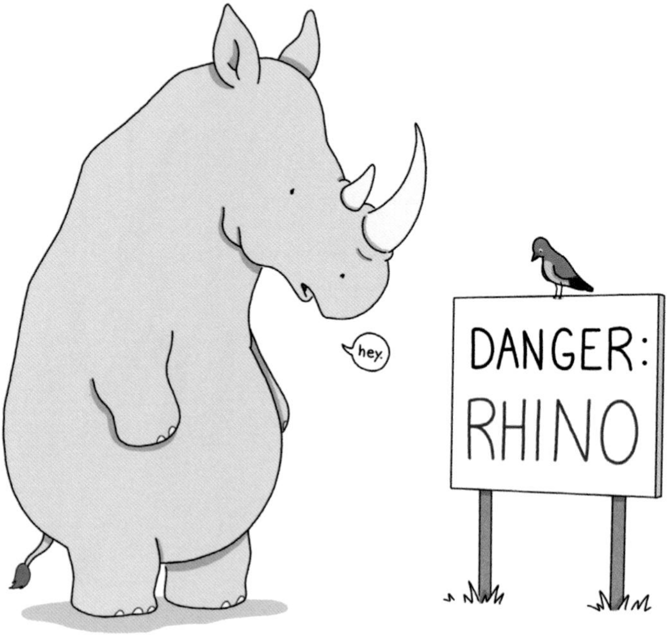
hey.
DANGER:
RHINO

Especially if

that someone is you.

Do *you* have that little voice in the back of your mind?

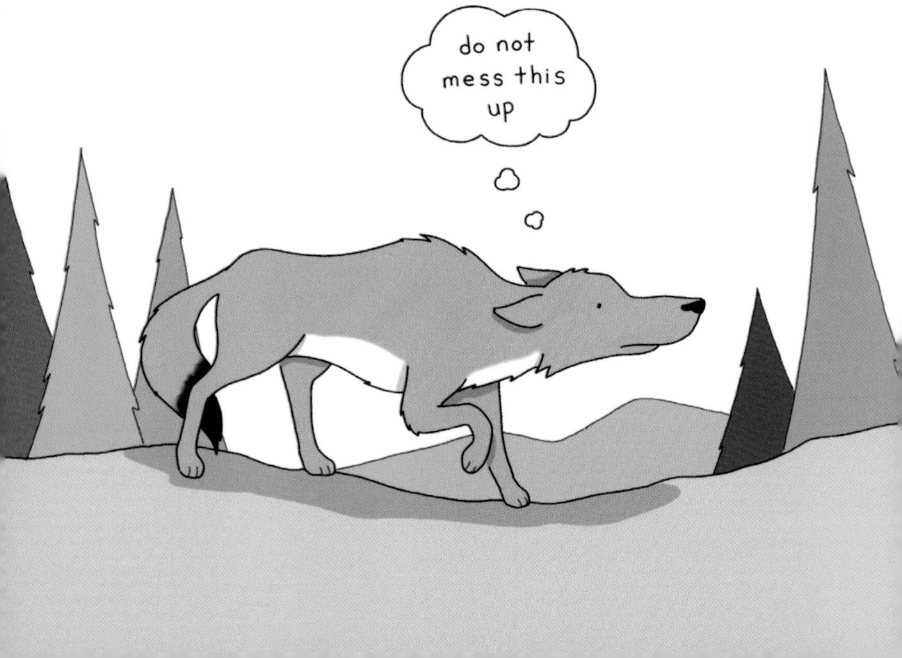
do not mess this up

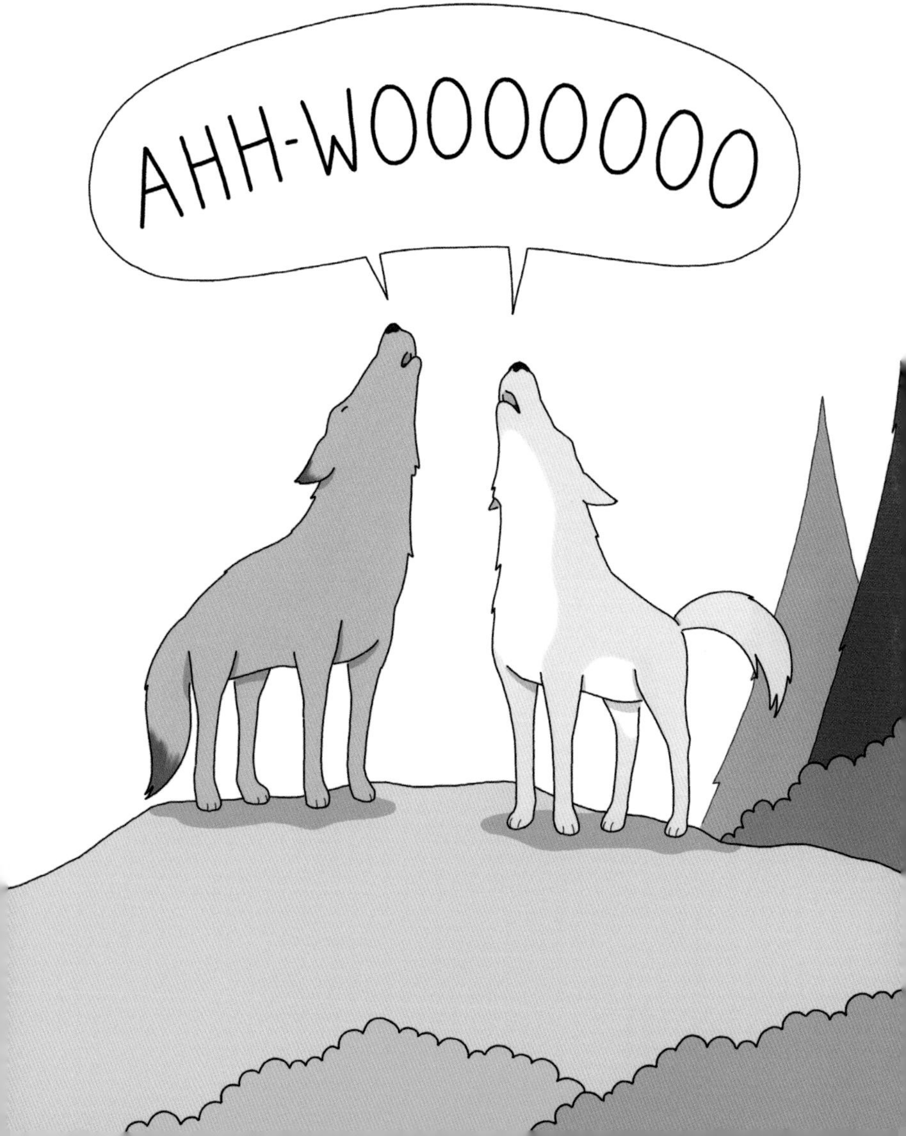
AHH-WOOOOOOO

It tells you to worry

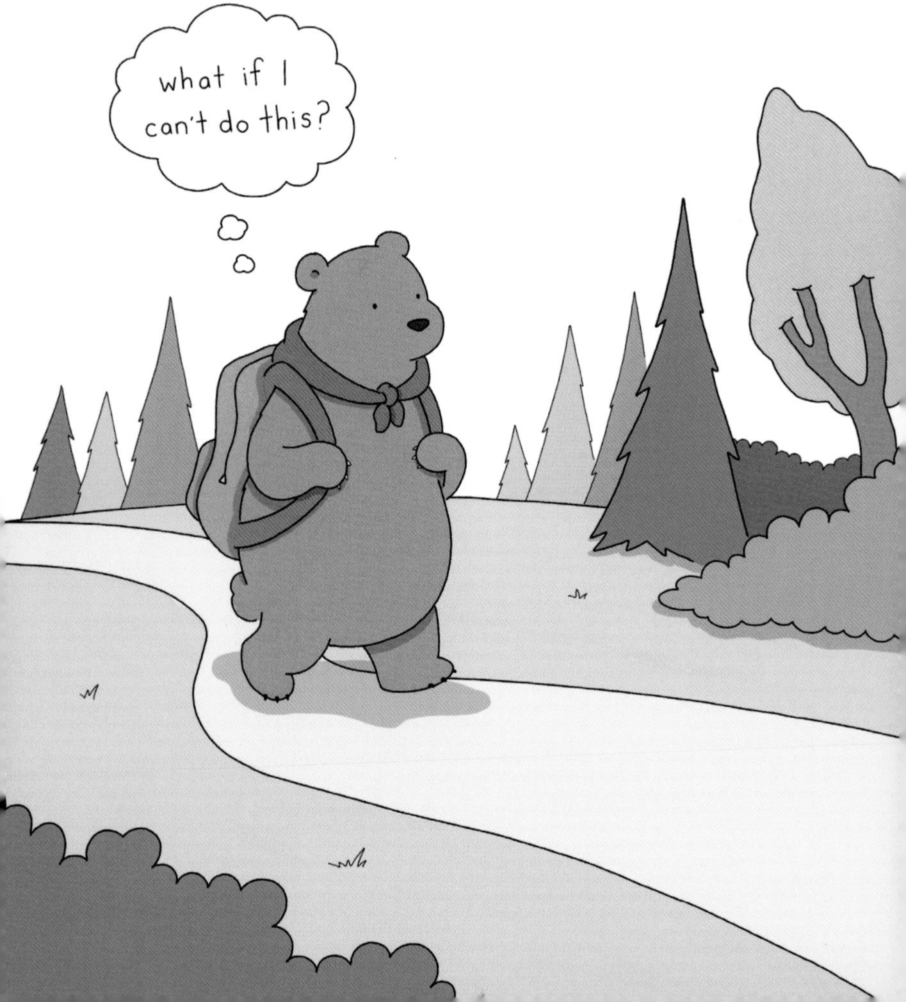
what if I can't do this?

and treats you unkind.

aw, crud.
you'll mess this up
this too.
past mistakes
failure
just give up and lay down

It says you can't do it.

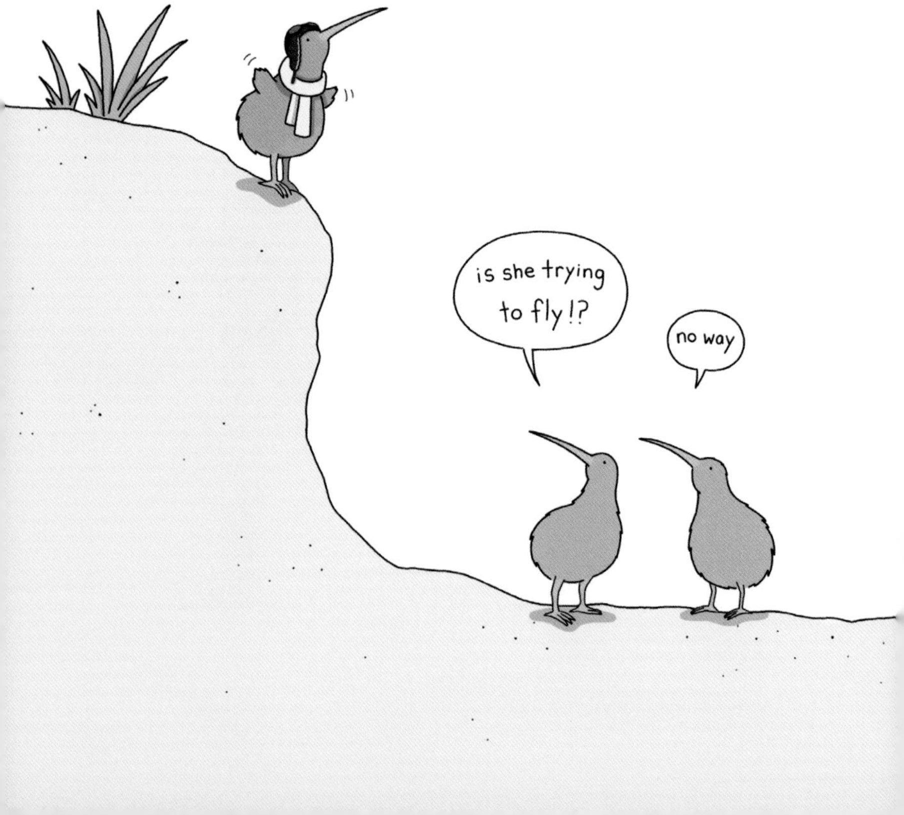
is she trying to fly!?
no way

It fills you with shame.

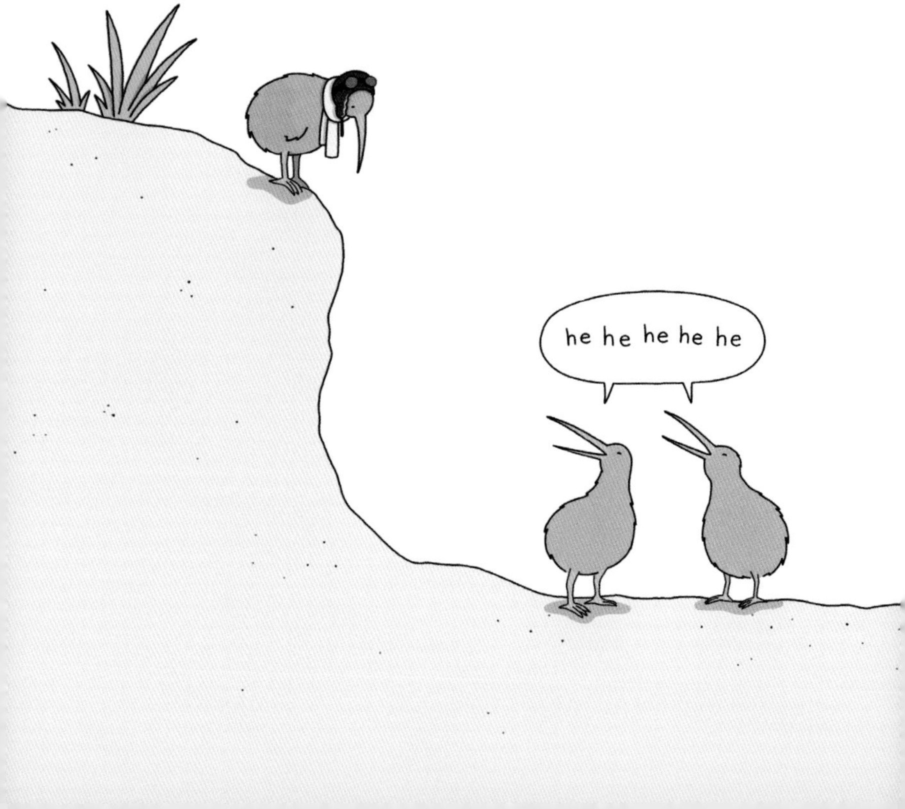
he he he he he

It says you'll mess up,
and that you'll be to blame.

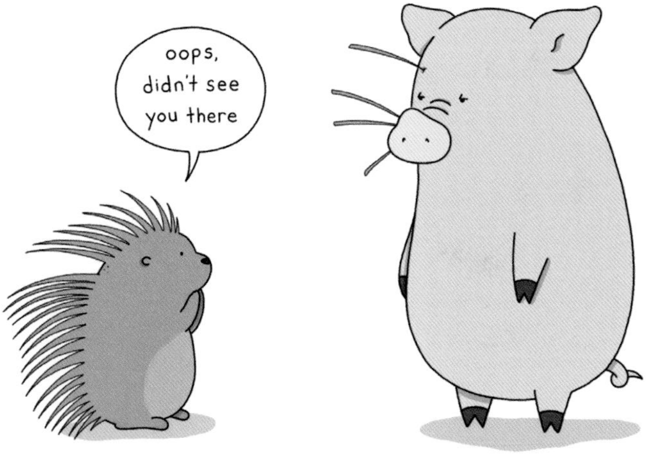
oops,
didn't see
you there

That voice is just fear, the baggage we carry.

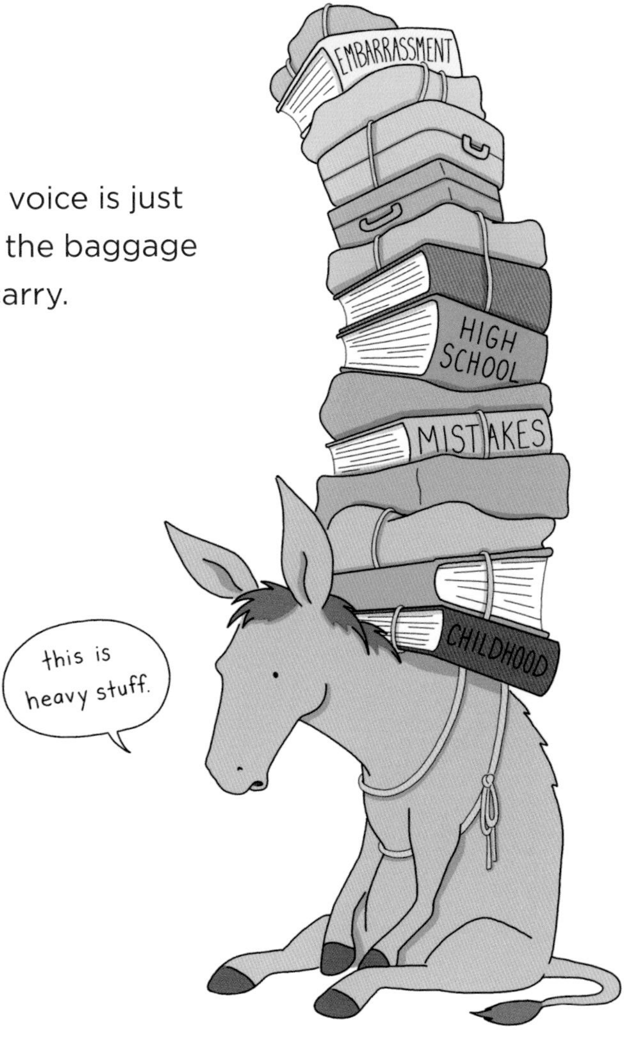
EMBARRASSMENT
HIGH SCHOOL
MISTAKES
CHILDHOOD
this is heavy stuff.

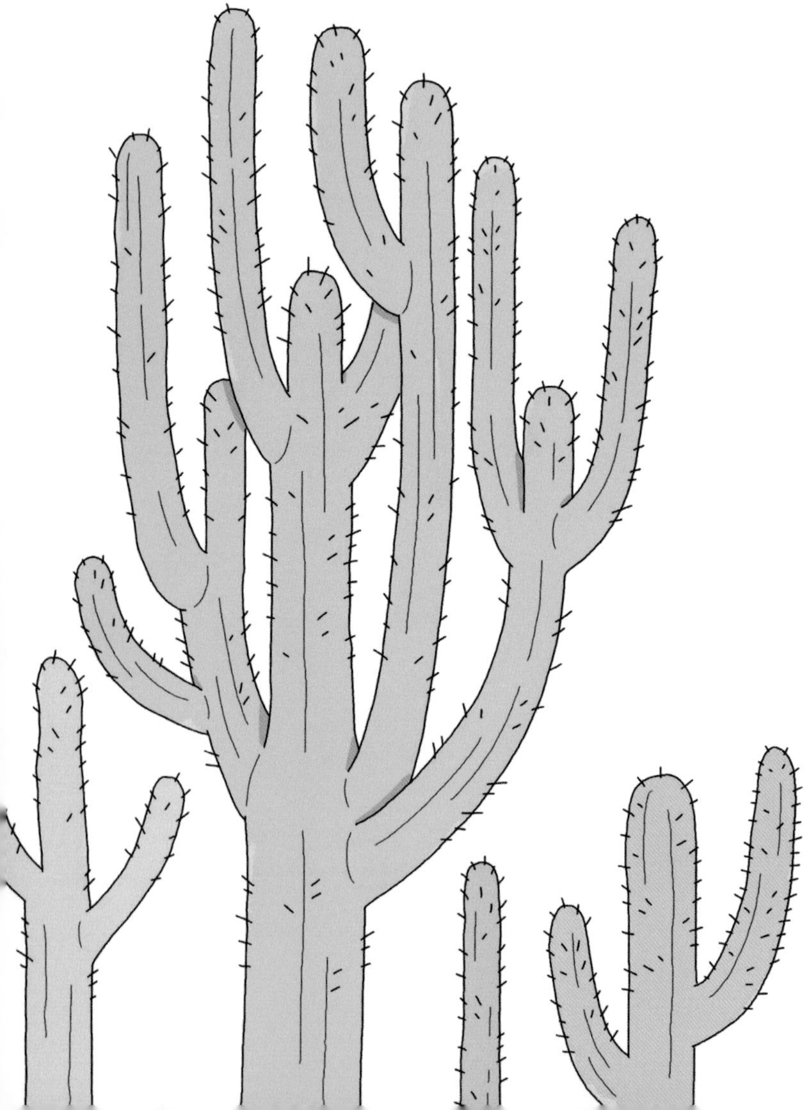

The mistakes of our past
making us wary.

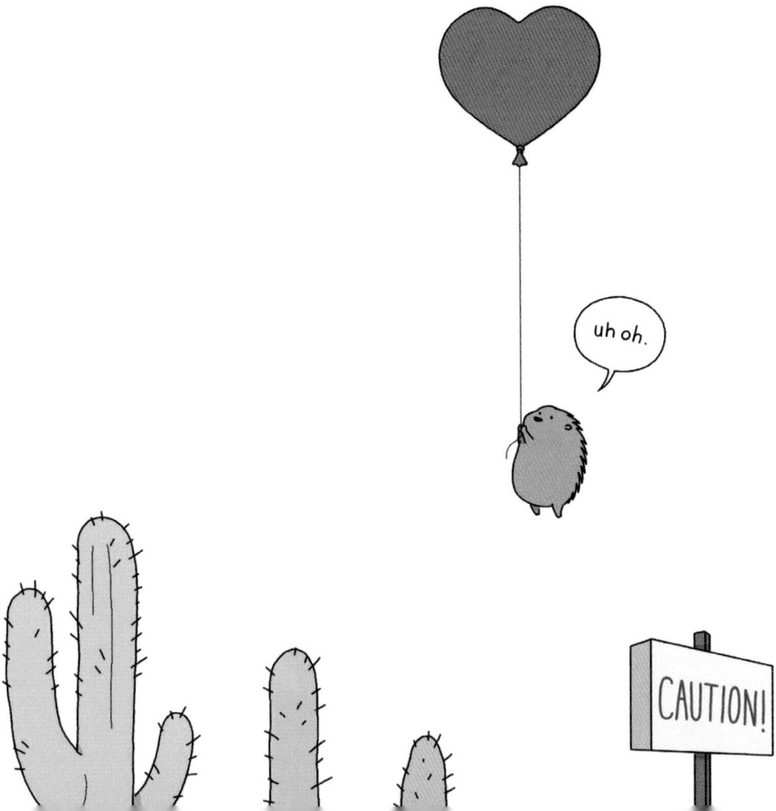
uh oh.
CAUTION!

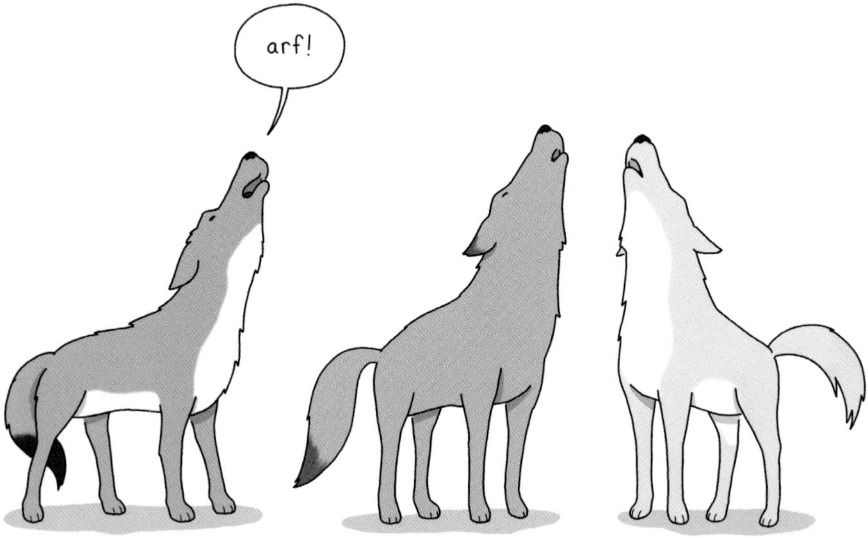
arf!

What if I told you

we *all* have self-doubt.

Decisions that scare us,

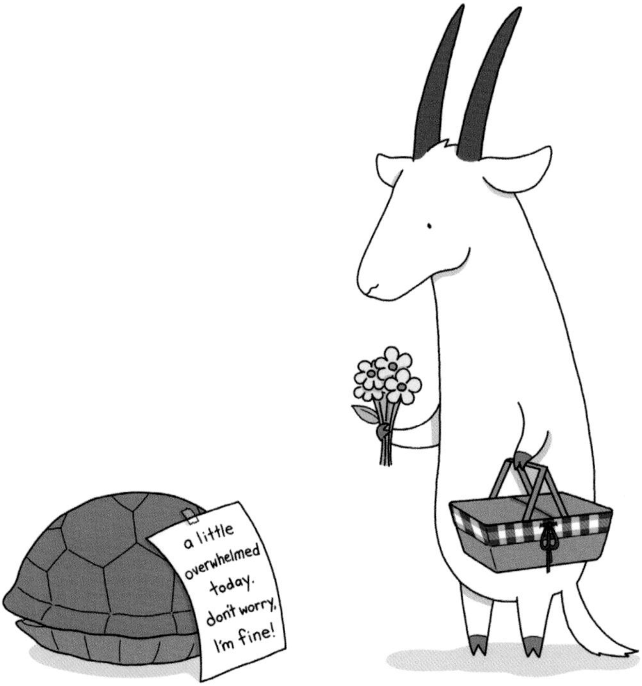
a little
overwhelmed
today.
don't worry,
I'm fine!

things we worry about.

Sometimes we
feel small.

Sometimes we
feel blue.

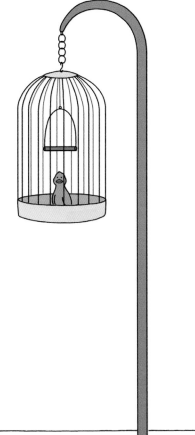

When we think of the future
our outlook's askew.

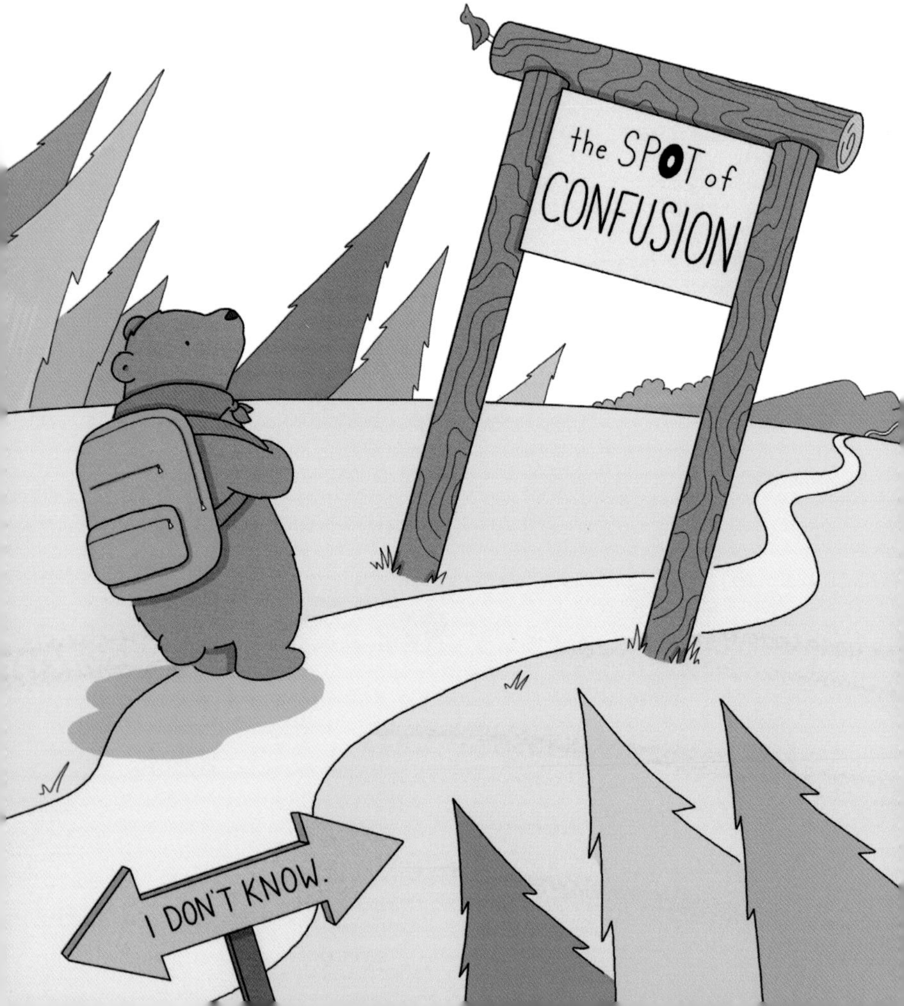
the SPOT of
CONFUSION
I DON'T KNOW.

We try to keep moving.
We're going nowhere.

We look for the bright side

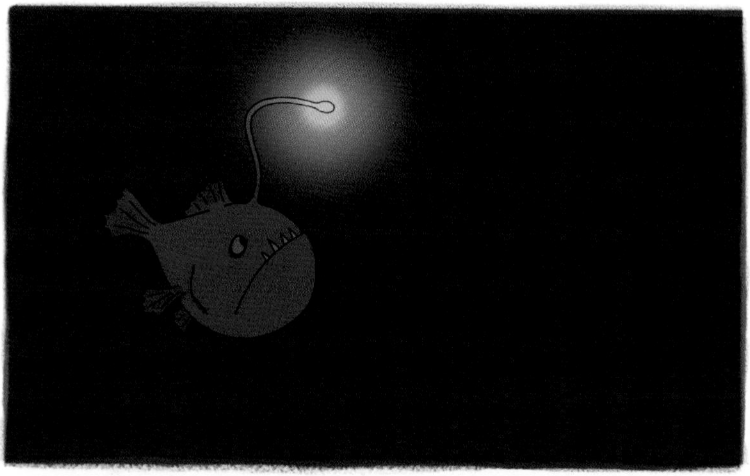

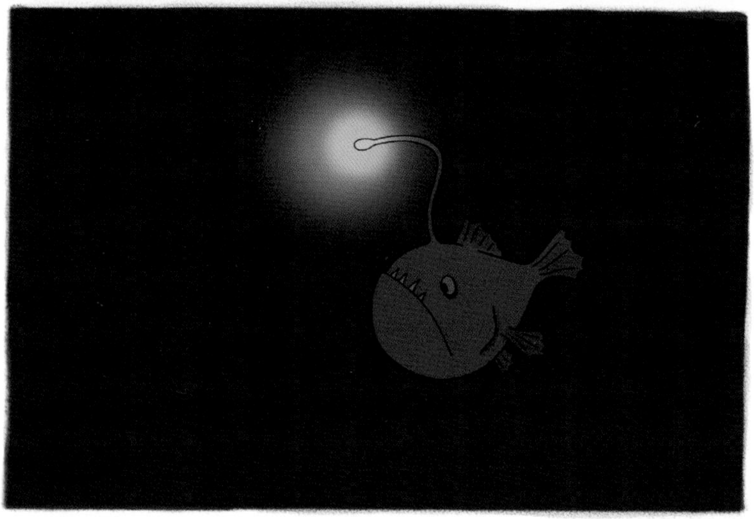

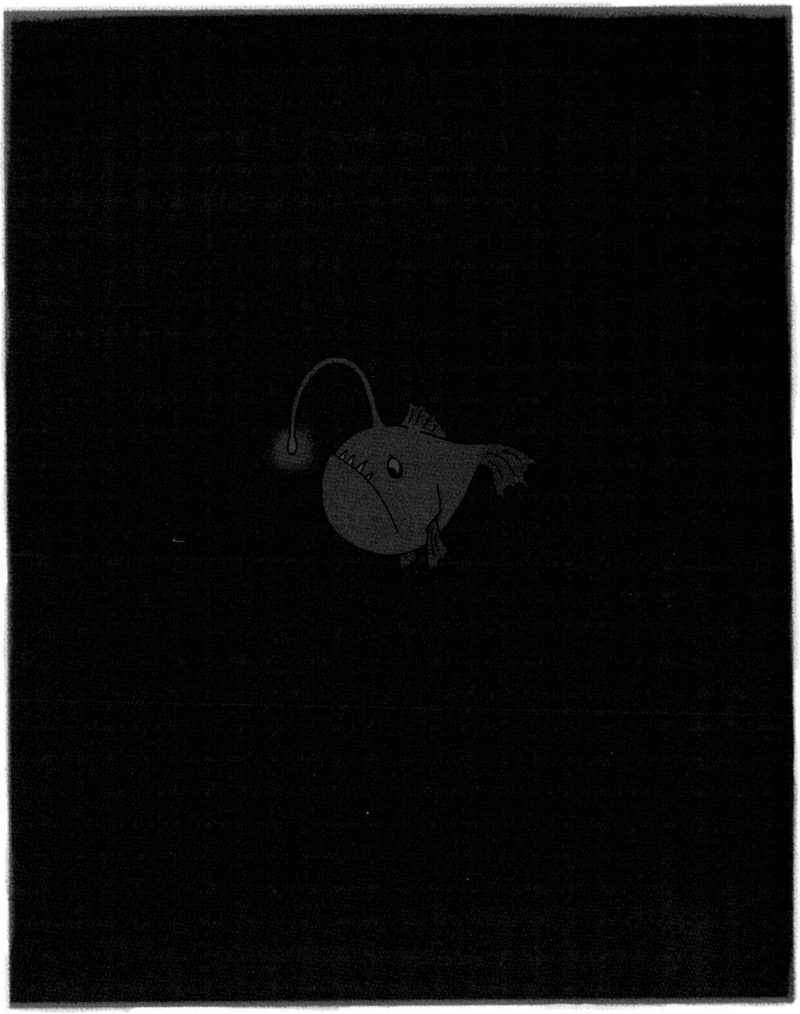

but it's dark everywhere.

Life can be *hard*.

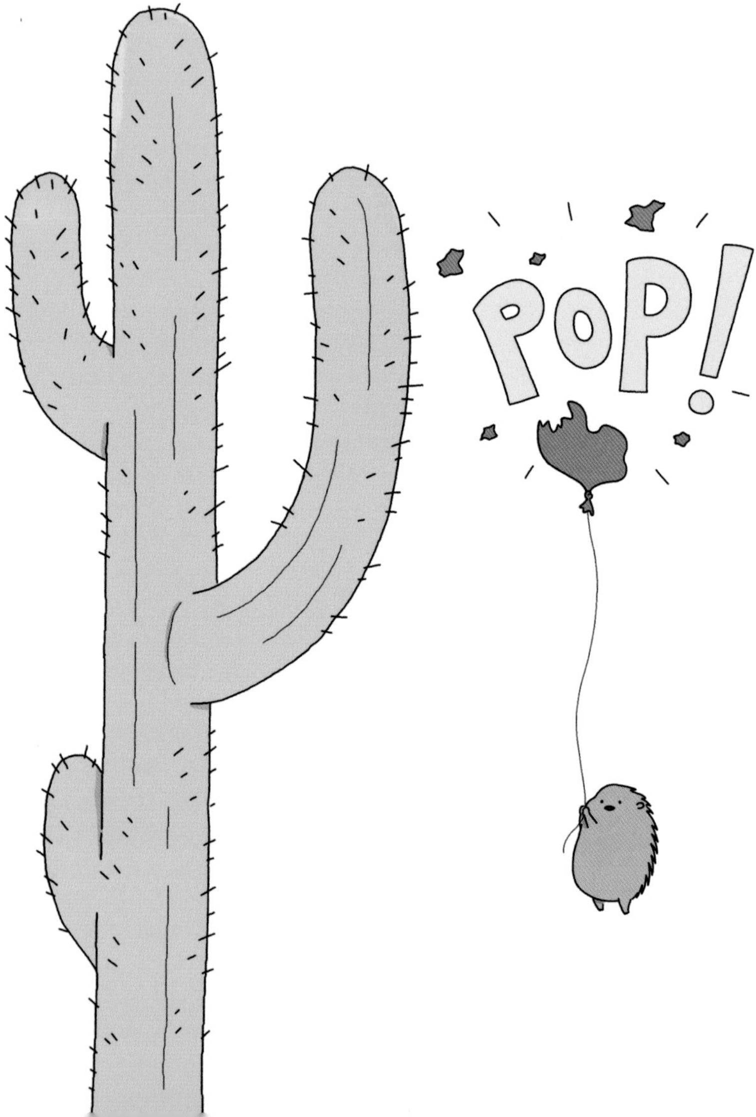
POP!

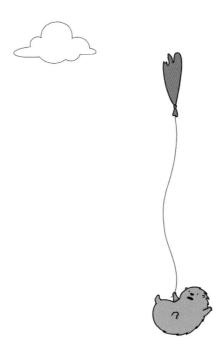

We've all felt this way.

Sometimes it's a challenge

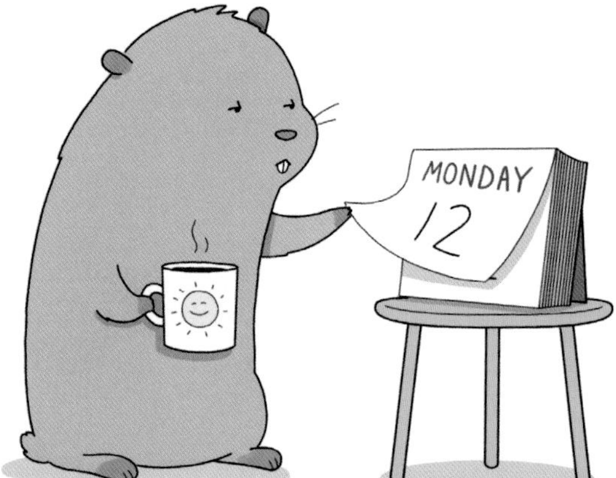
MONDAY
12

just to get through the day.

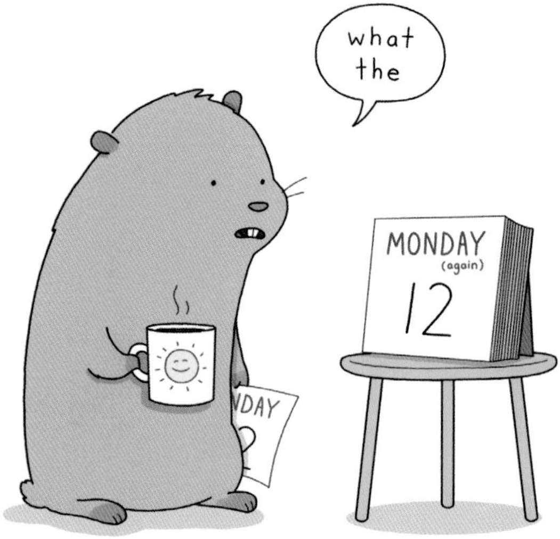
what the
MONDAY
(again)
12
DAY

But trust me,
you've got this!

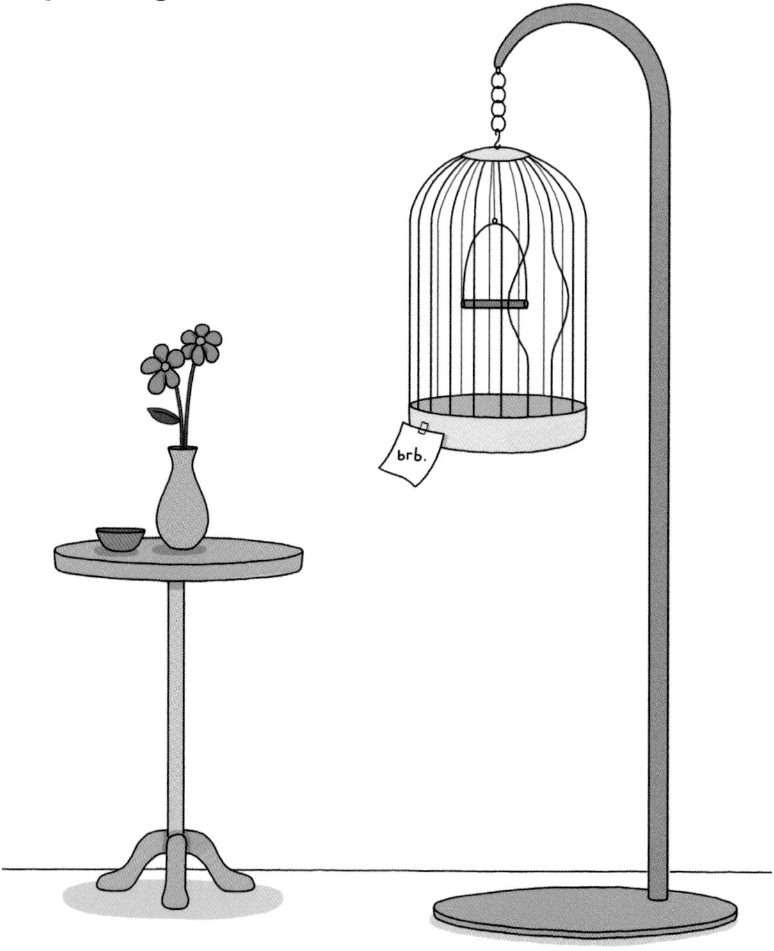
brb.

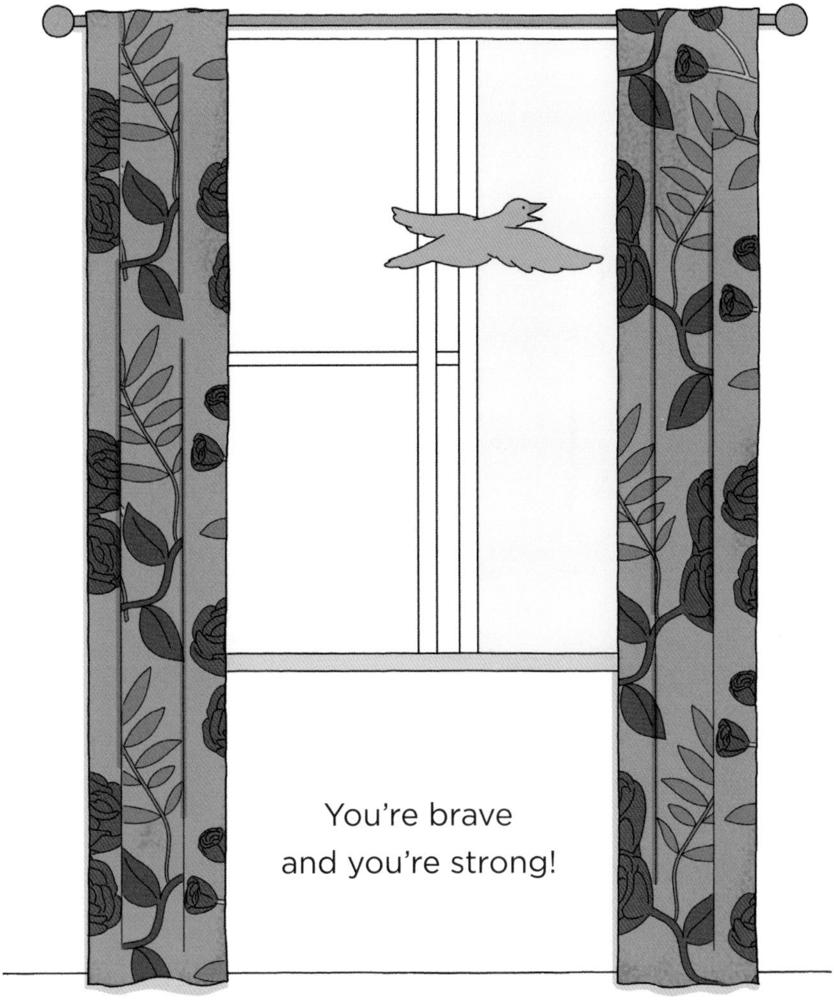

You're brave
and you're strong!

And if someone disagrees

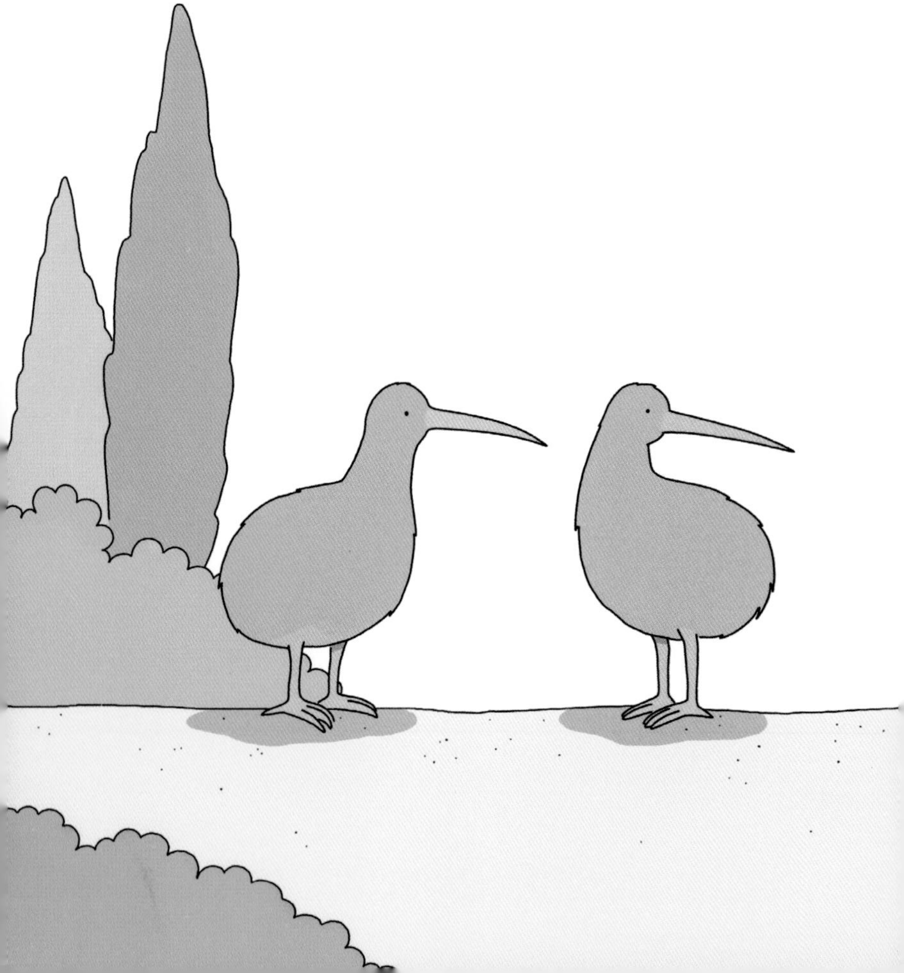

you can just move along.

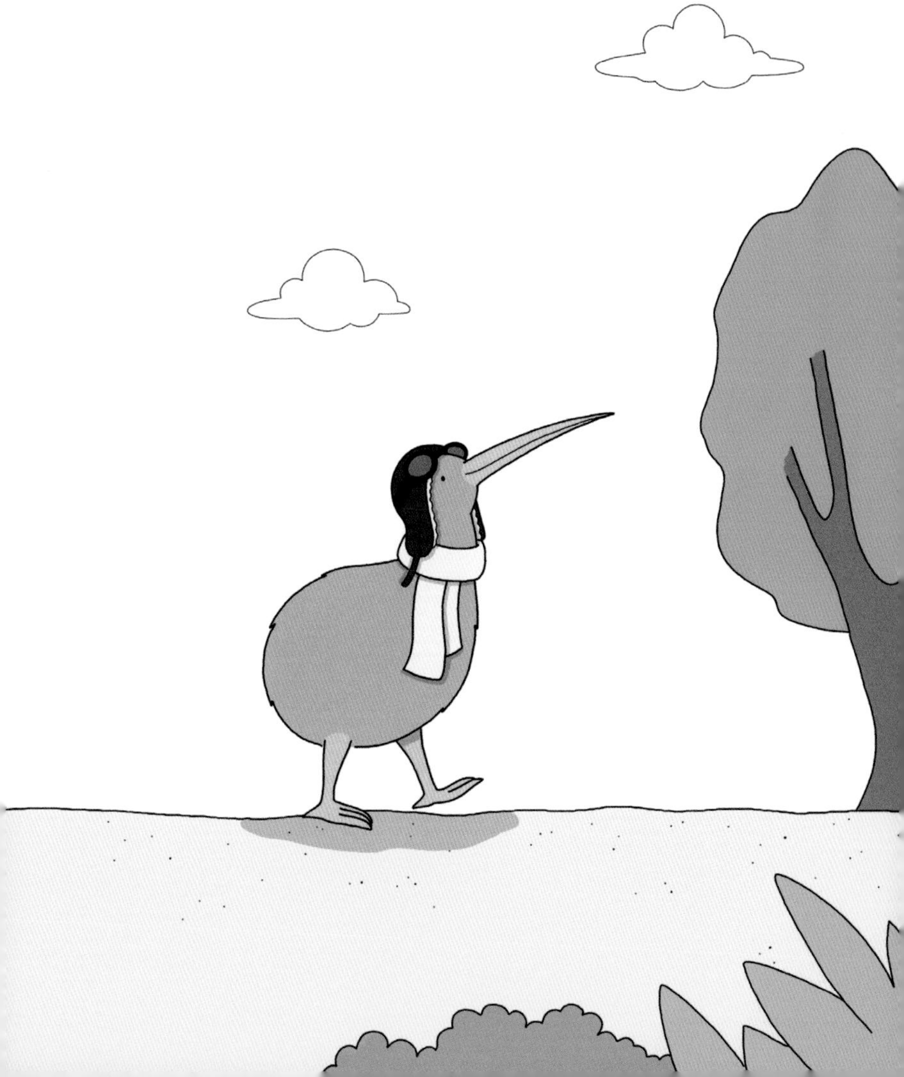

Not everyone's for you

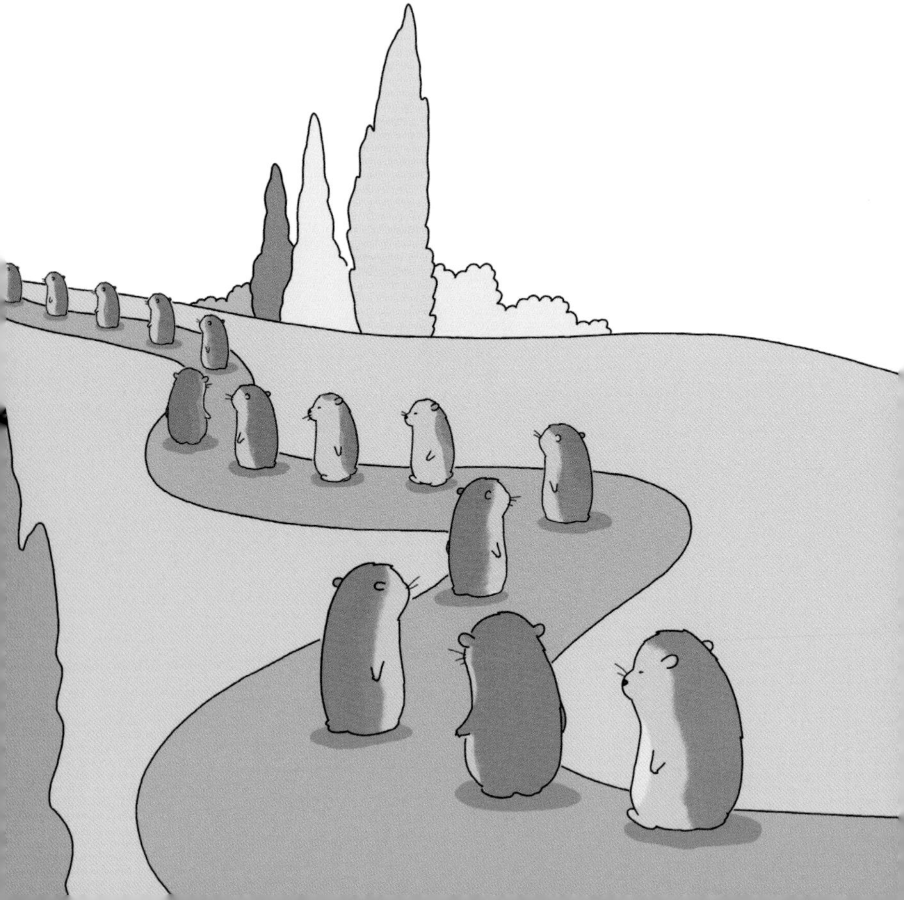

and that's okay!

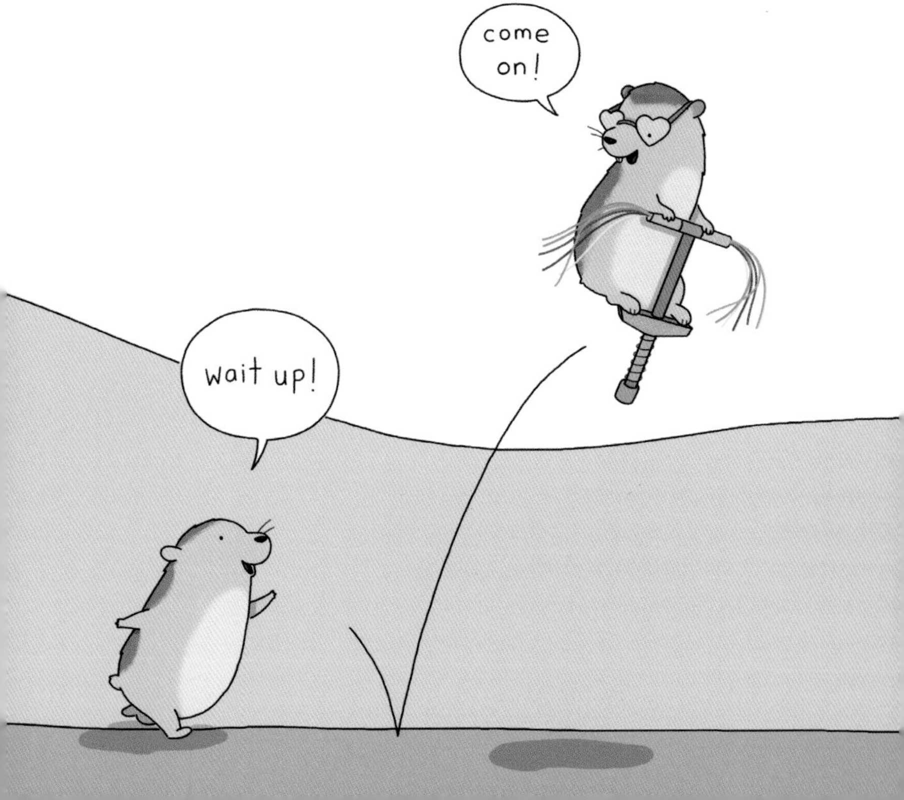
come on!
wait up!

If something doesn't
serve you

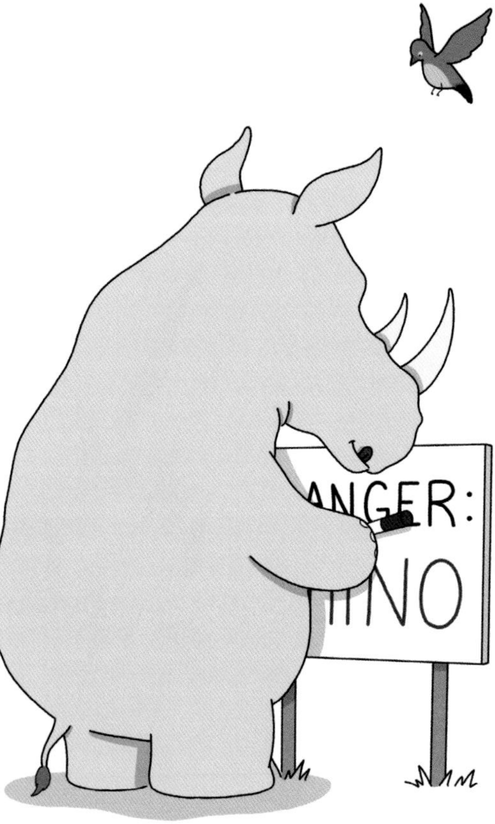
ANGER:
NO

just send it on its way.

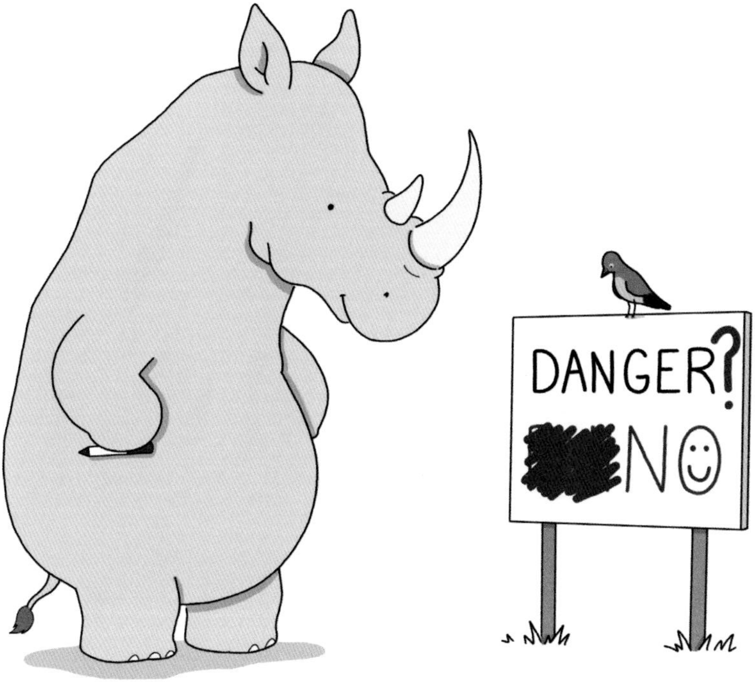
DANGER?
[redacted] NO

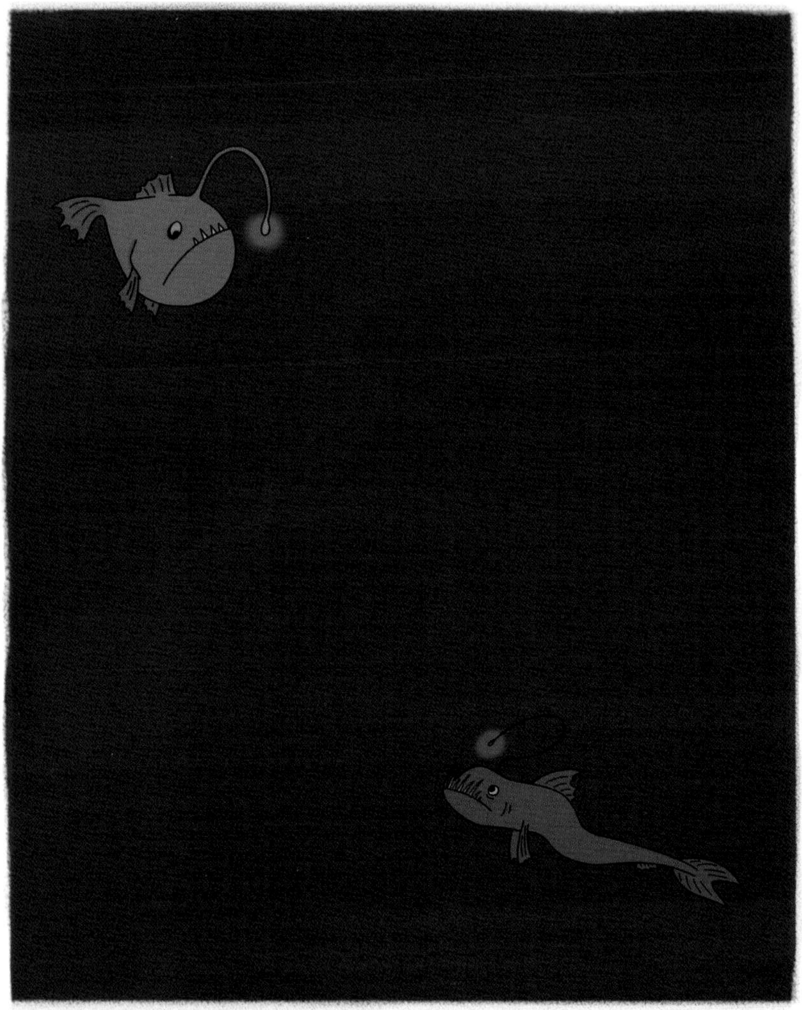

Make room for the people

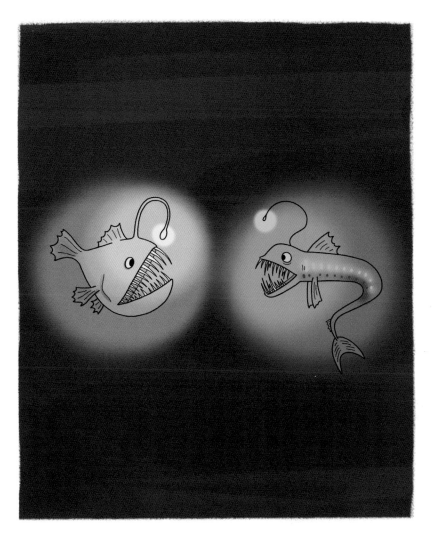

who see how you *shine*.

Who show up when you need them

even when you aren't fine.

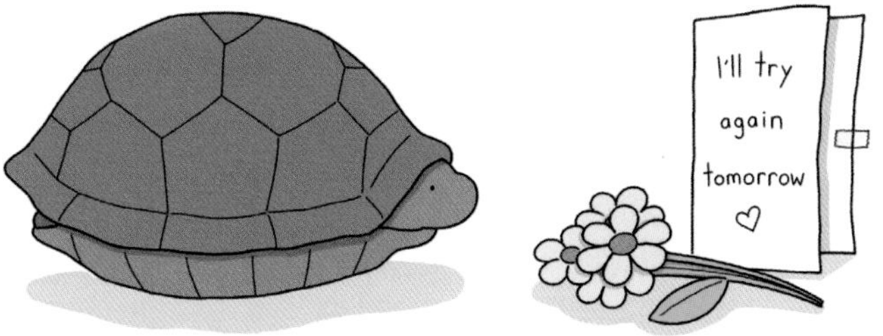
I'll try
again
tomorrow

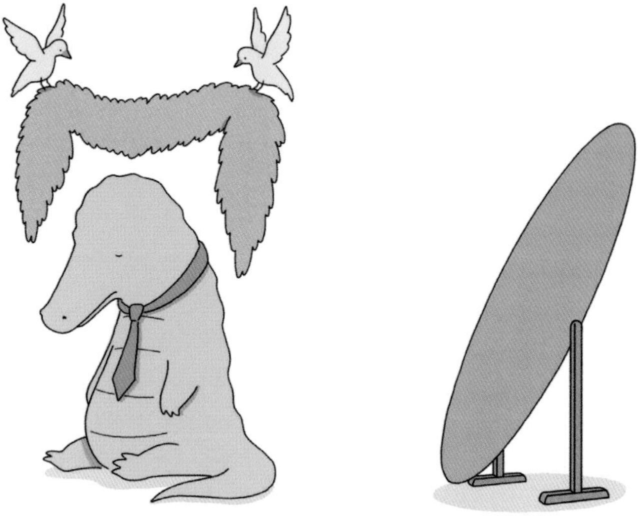

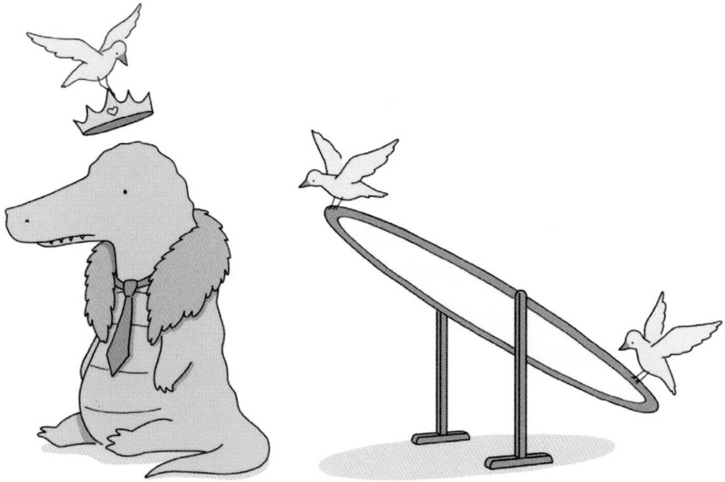

You know who you are.

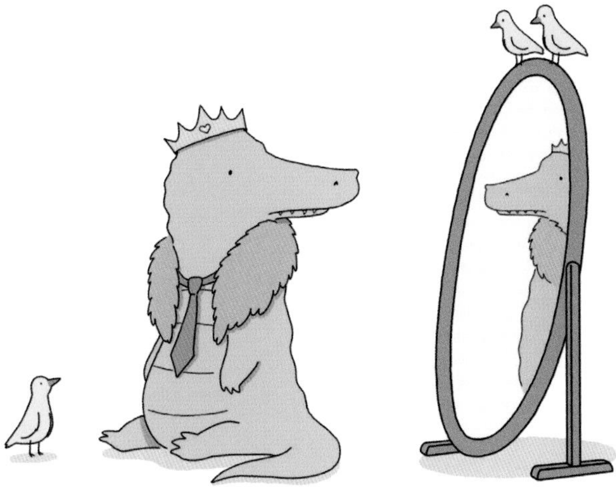

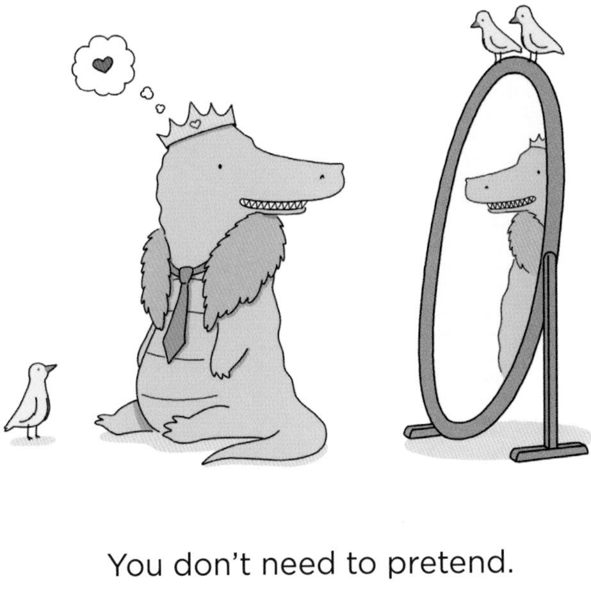

You don't need to pretend.

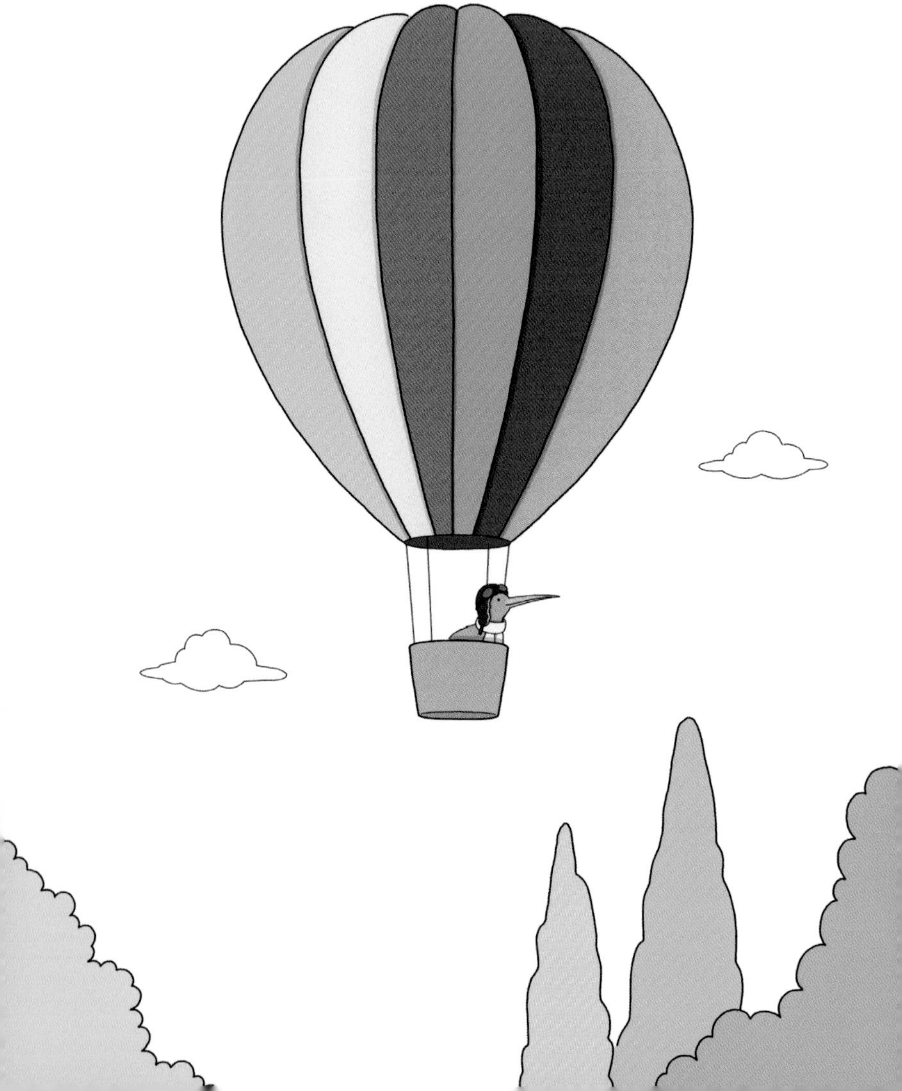

Or put yourself down
to appease a false
friend.

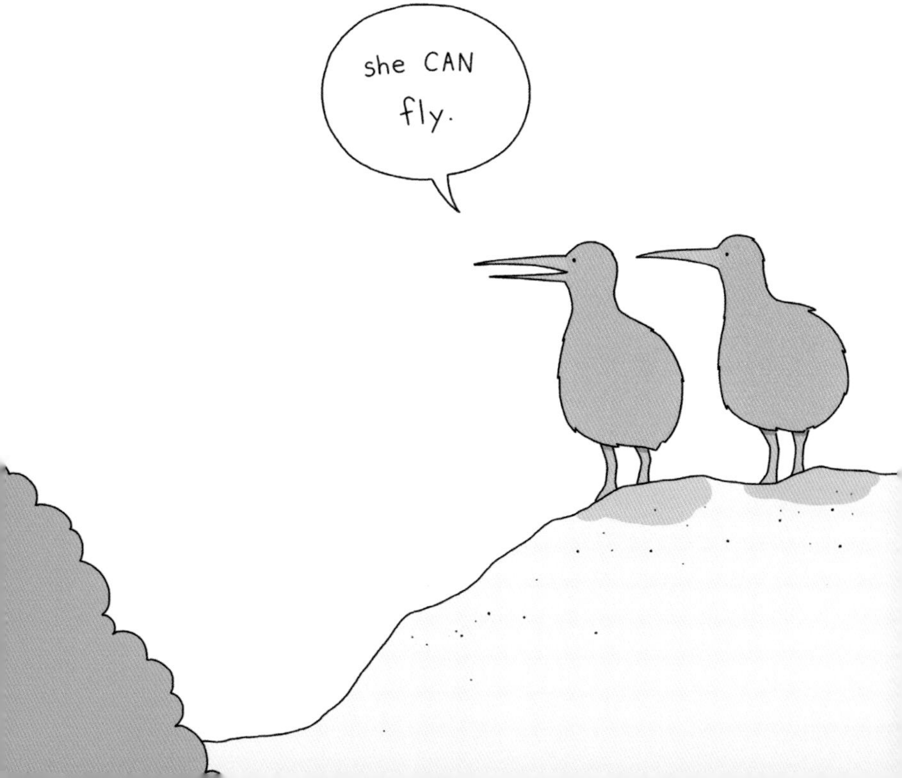
she CAN fly.

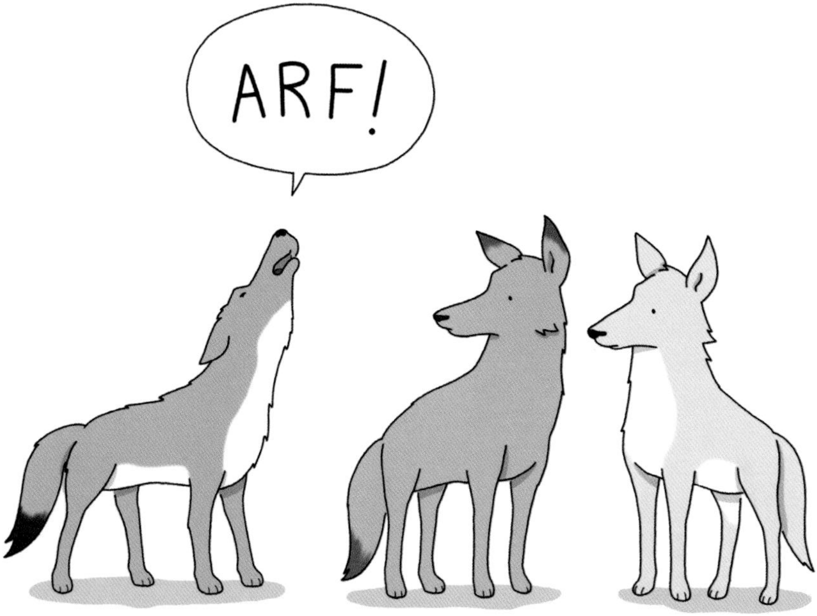
ARF!

Embrace all the good things

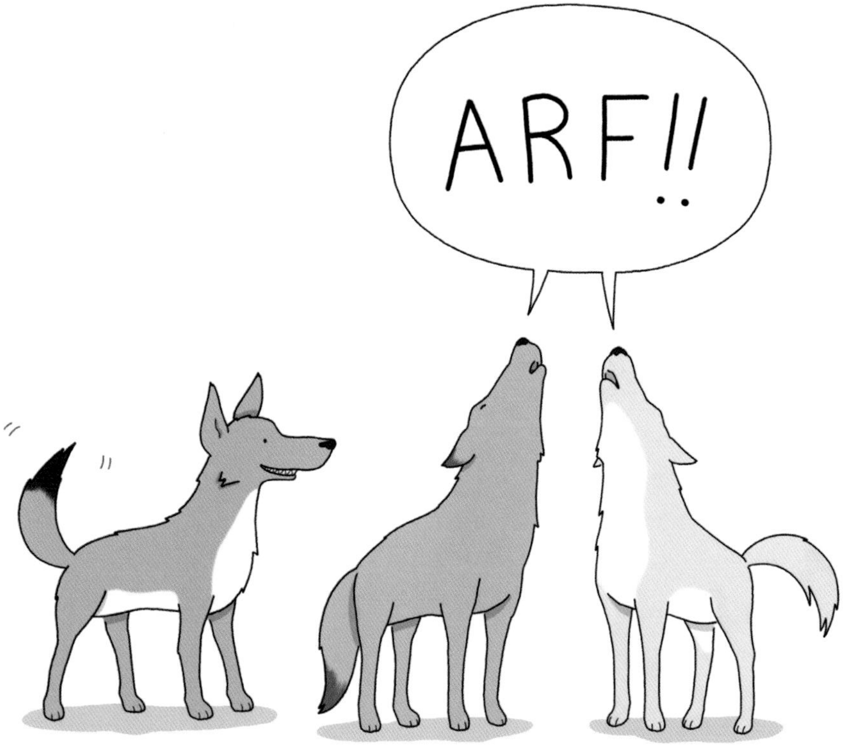
ARF!!

you see in yourself.

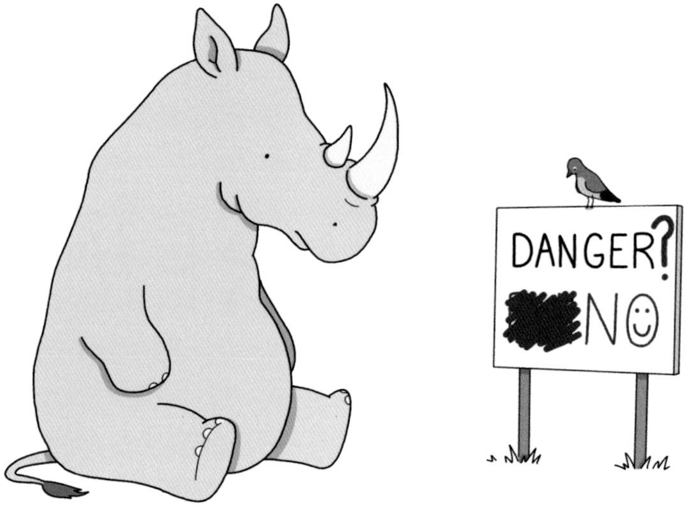
DANGER?
[redacted] NO

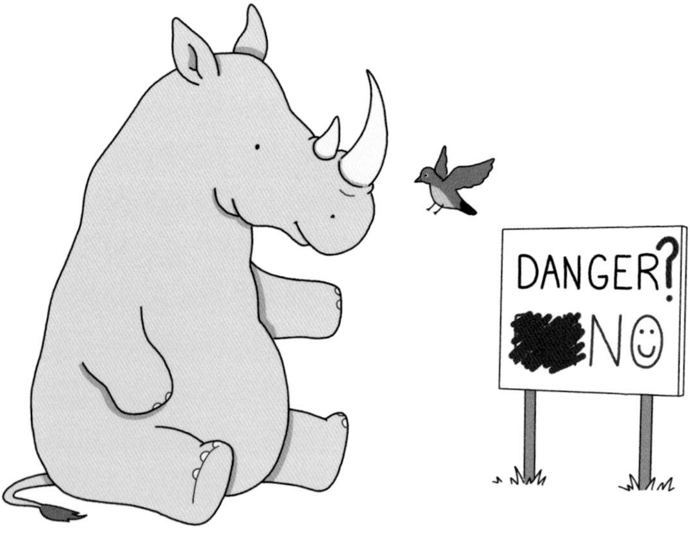
DANGER?
[redacted] NO

You deserve the same kindness
you show everyone else.

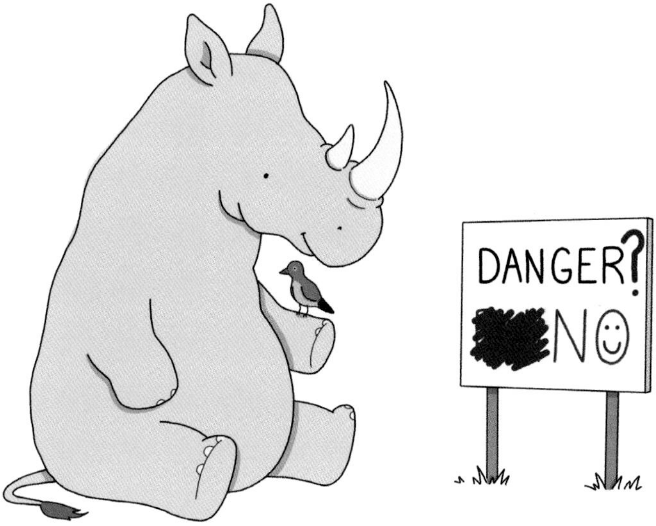
DANGER?
[redacted] NO

Now, this part is important

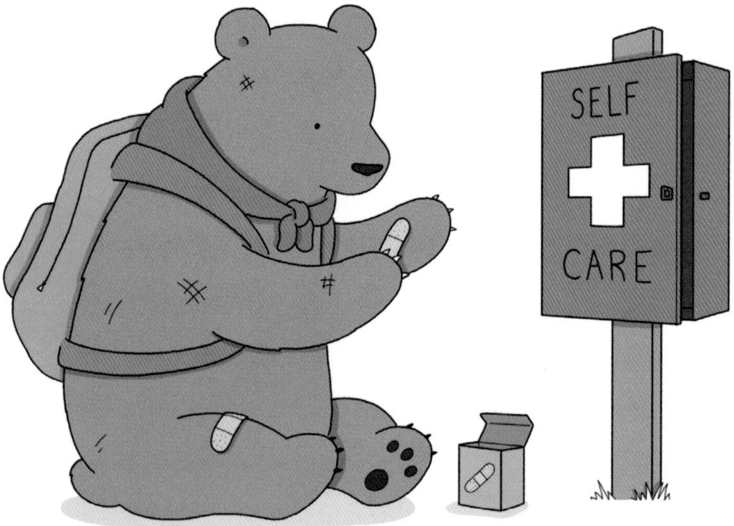
SELF
CARE

so please pay attention:

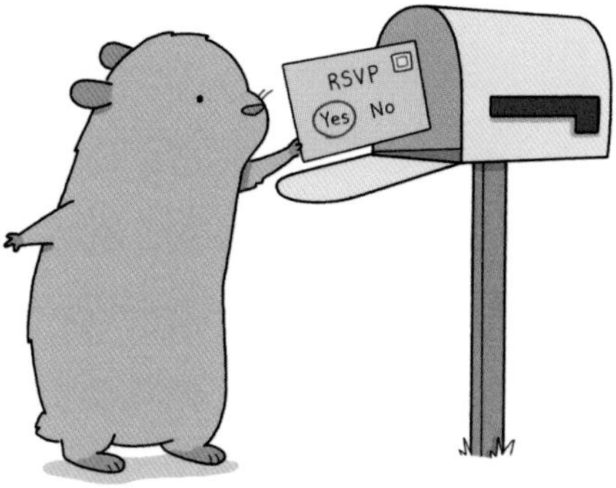
RSVP
Yes No

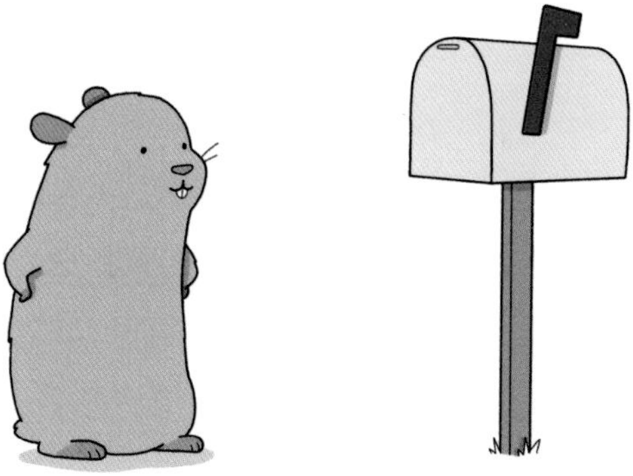

The hard things in your past,
those mistakes that I mentioned?

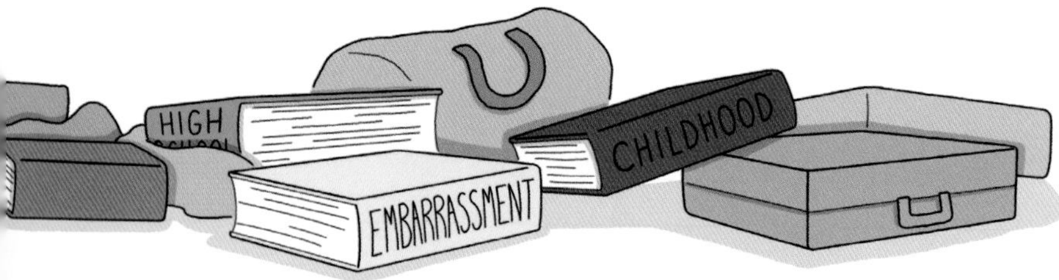
HIGH
CHILDHOOD
EMBARRASSMENT

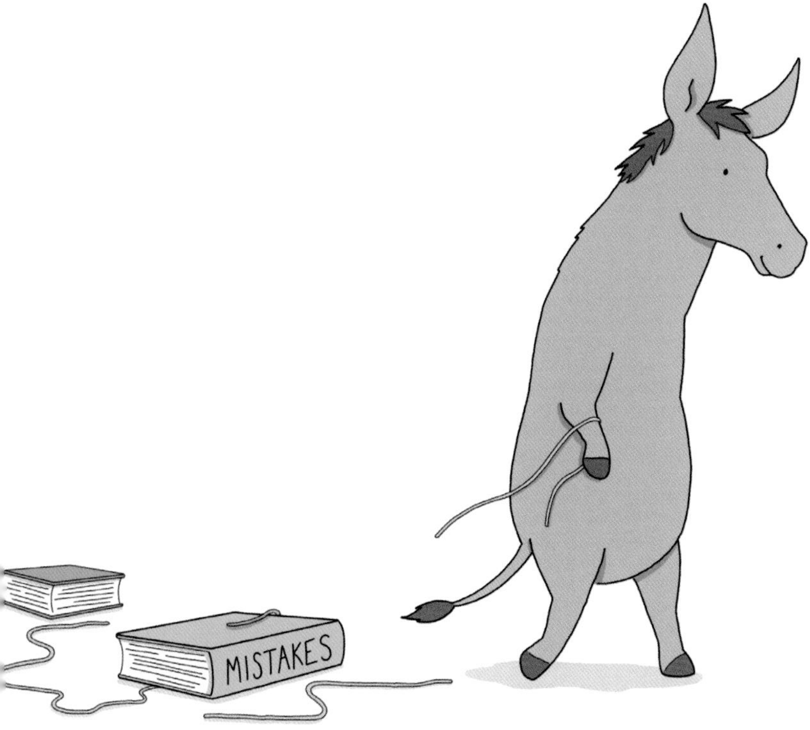
MISTAKES

They helped to make you

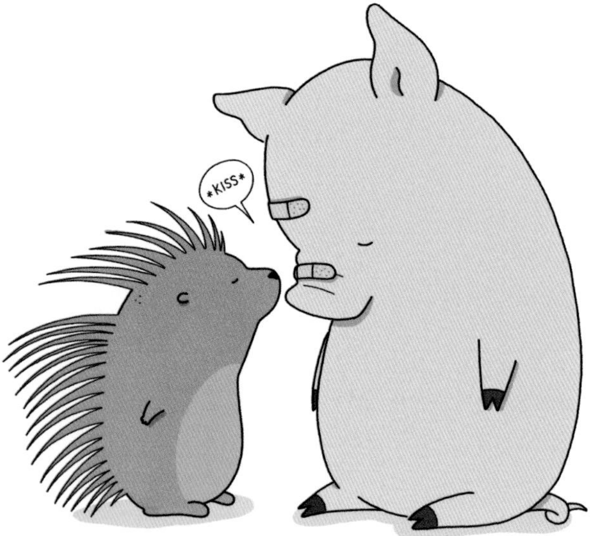
KISS

the person you are.

You've been
through a lot

thanks!
you too!

hey
nice flying!

and you've come really far!

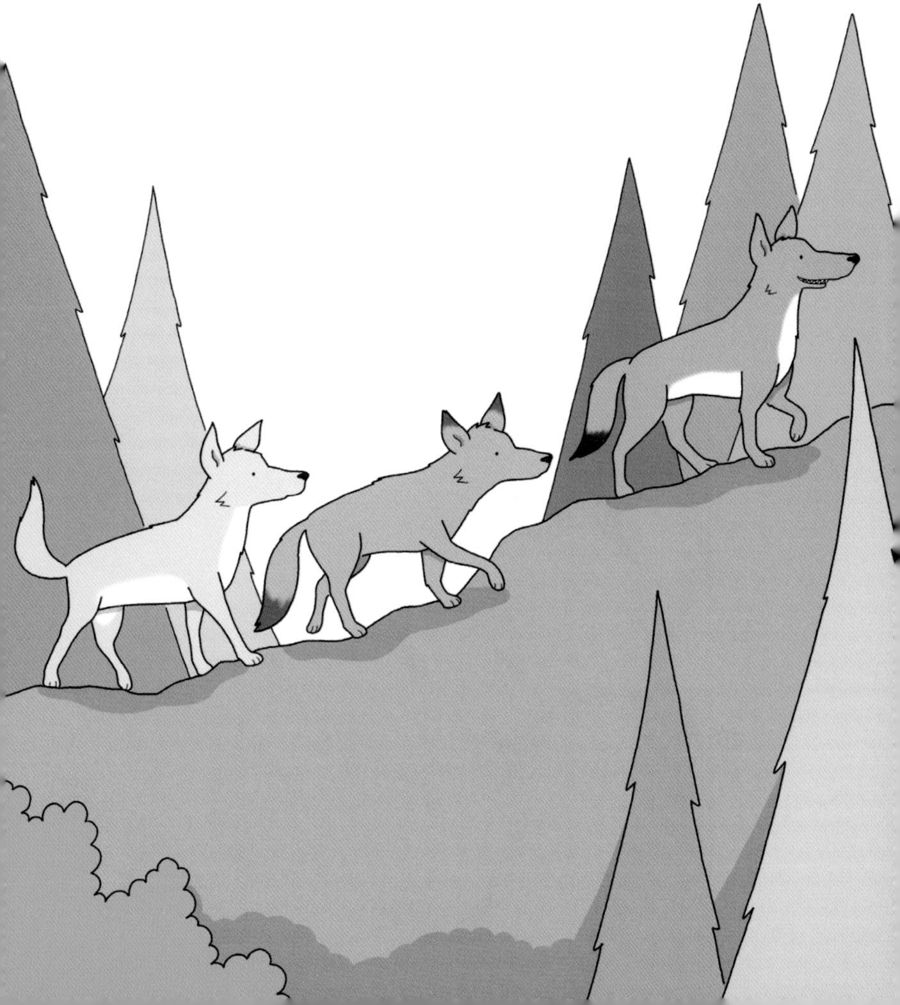

So if your day is tough,
if you slip and you fall,

if you've messed something up,
or can't deal with it all

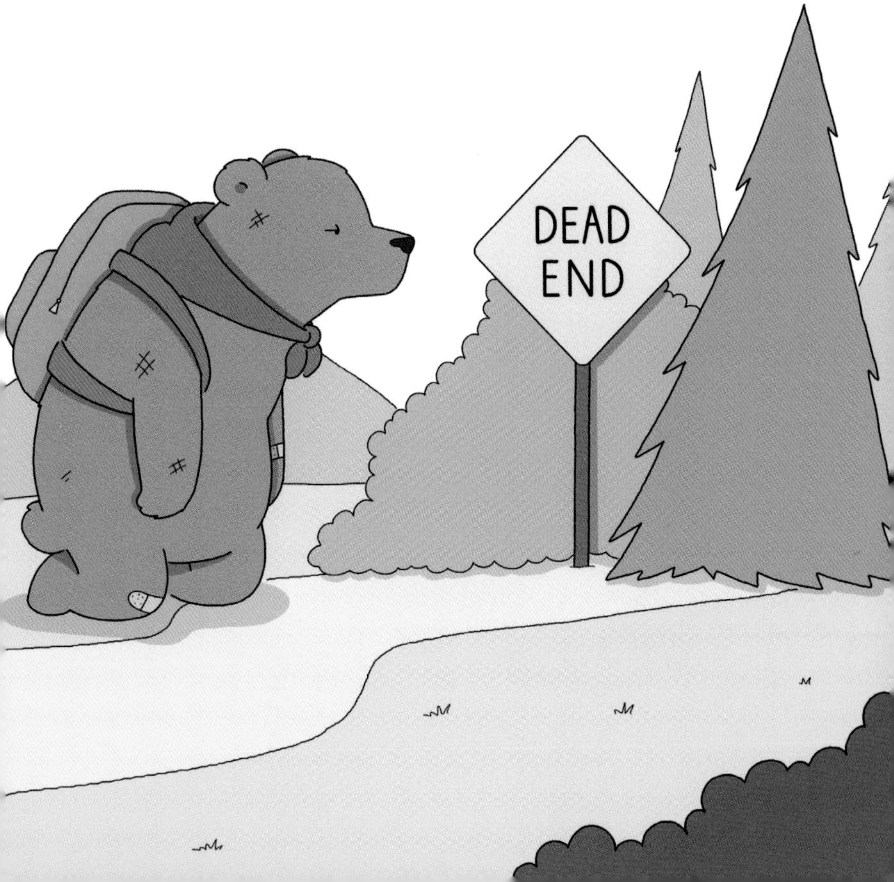
DEAD
END

remember that failing is how
you keep growing.

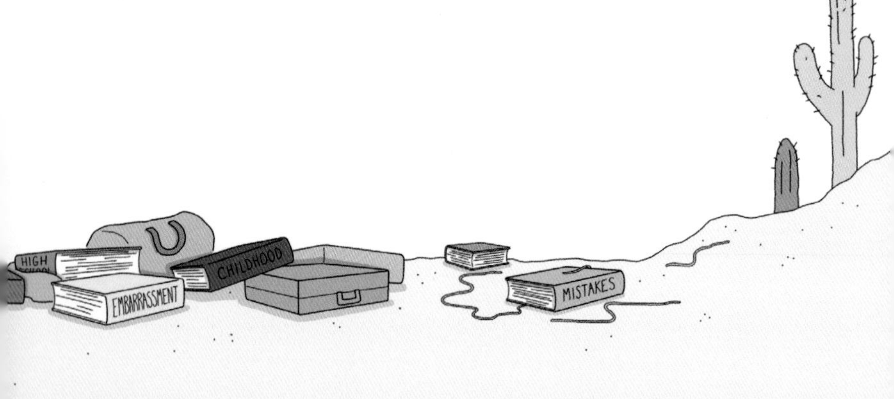
HIGH
CHILDHOOD
EMBARRASSMENT
MISTAKES

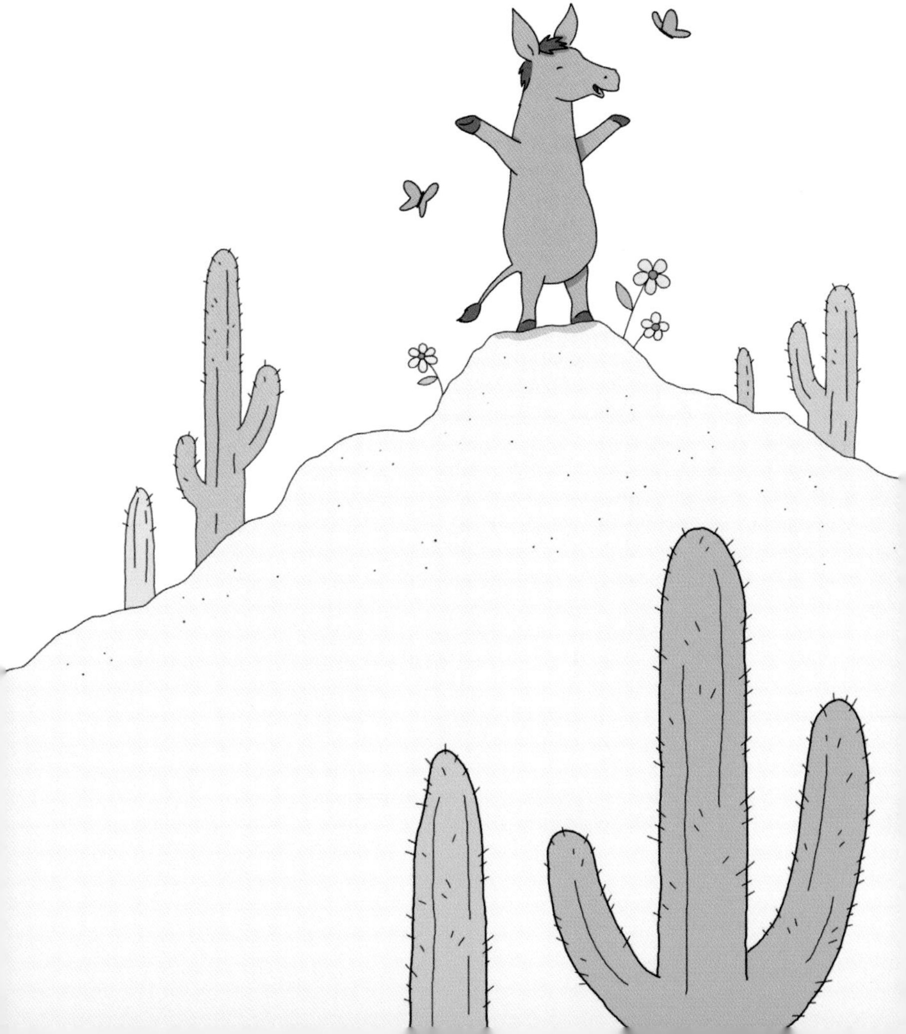

Be patient with yourself

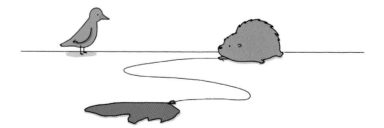

and try to keep going.

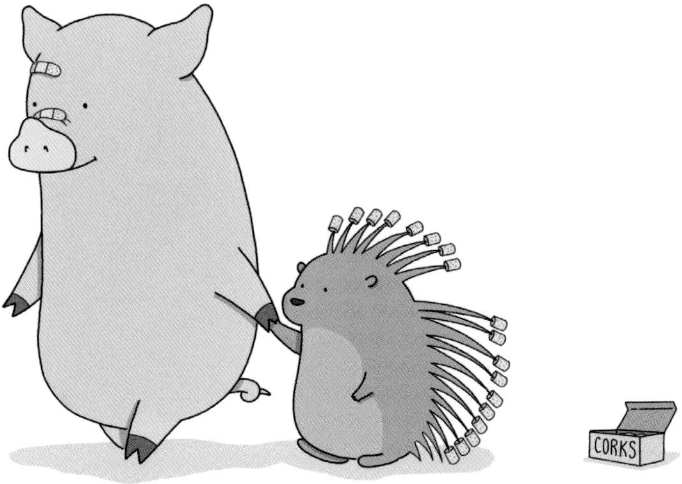
CORKS

Just keep moving forward

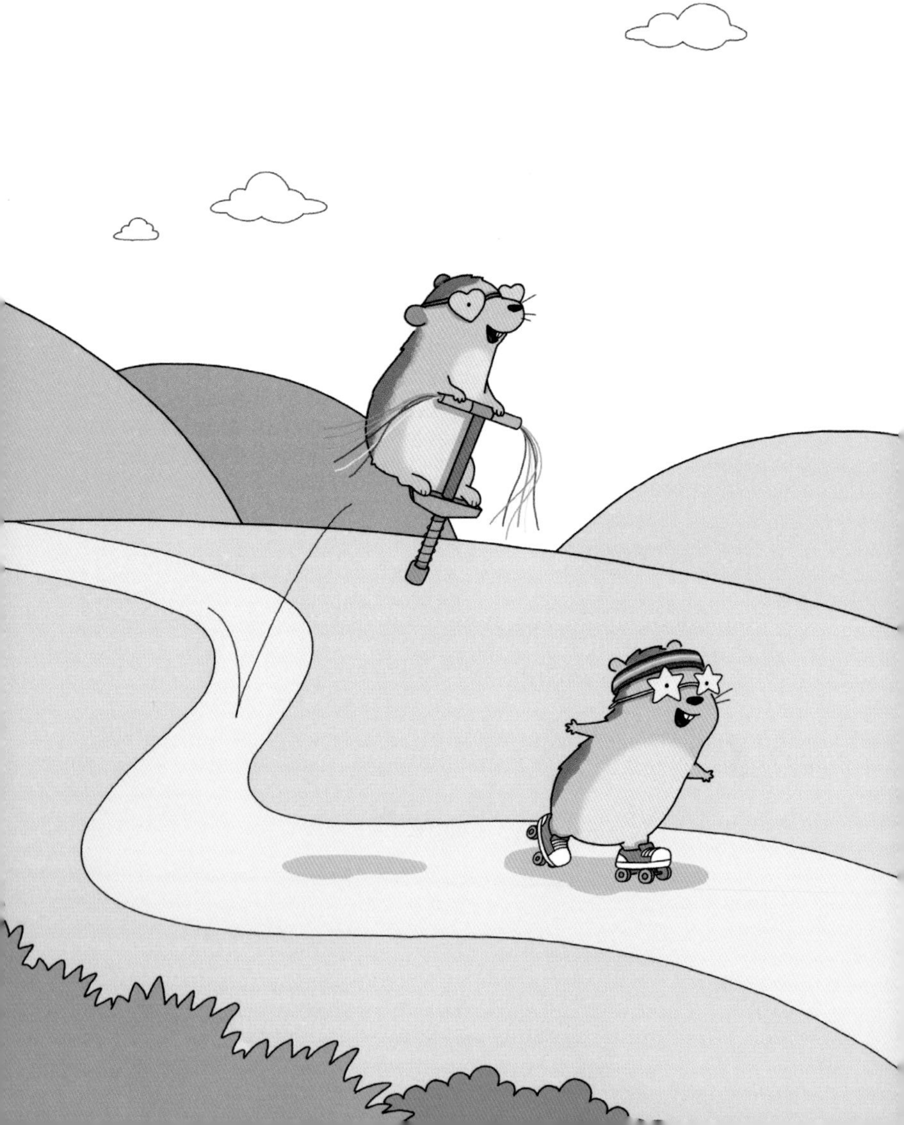

and do your very best

to accept those who mean you well and
pay no mind to the rest.

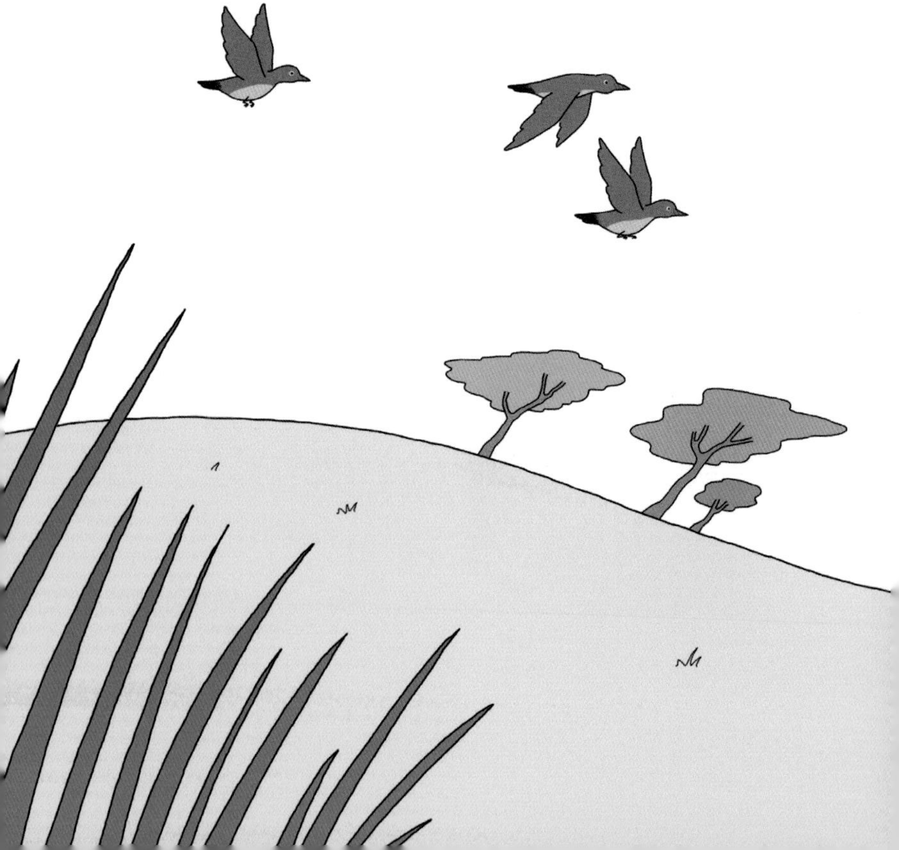

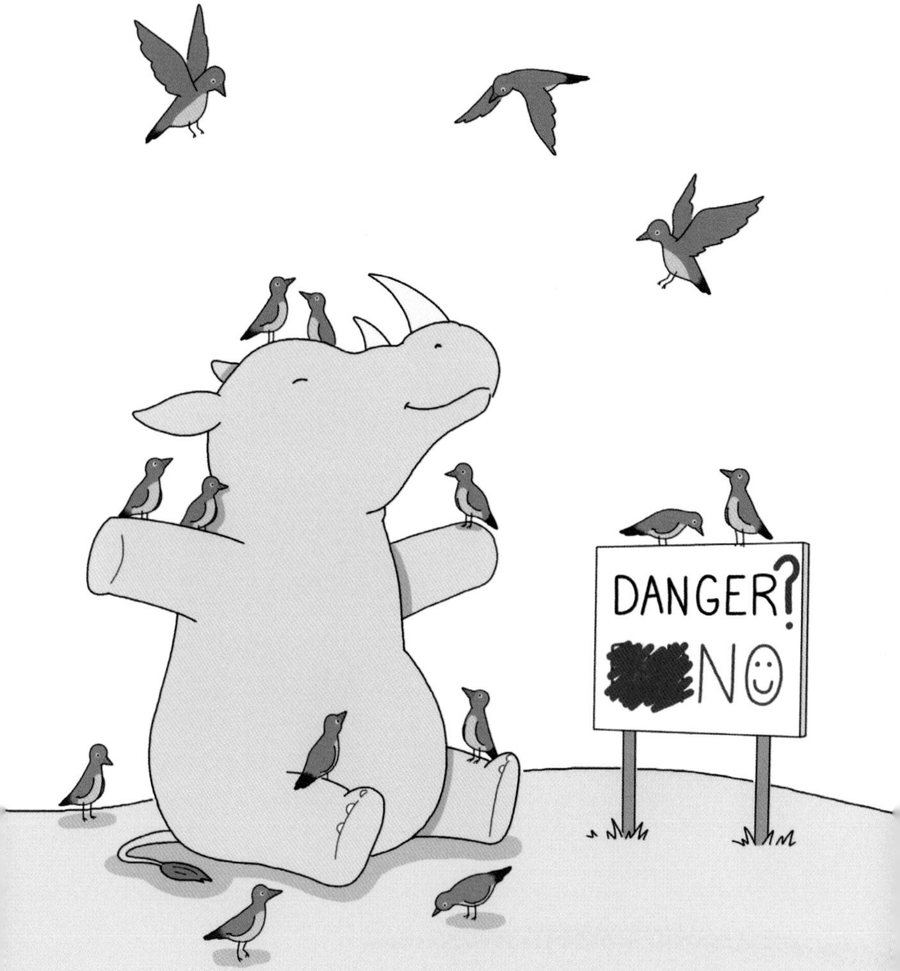
DANGER?
[redacted] NO

And when things feel impossible,

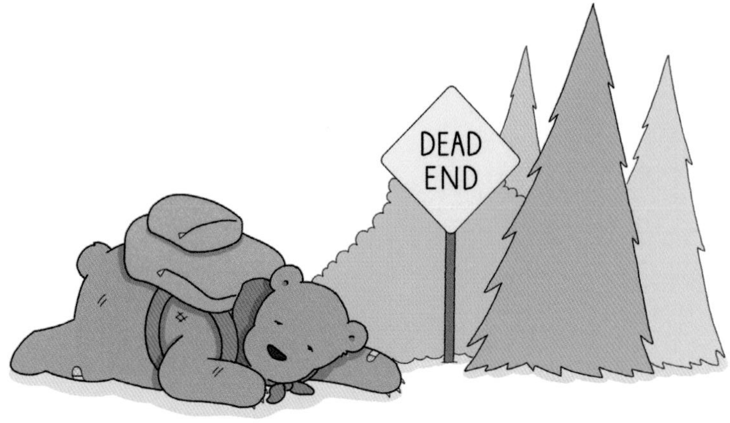
DEAD
END

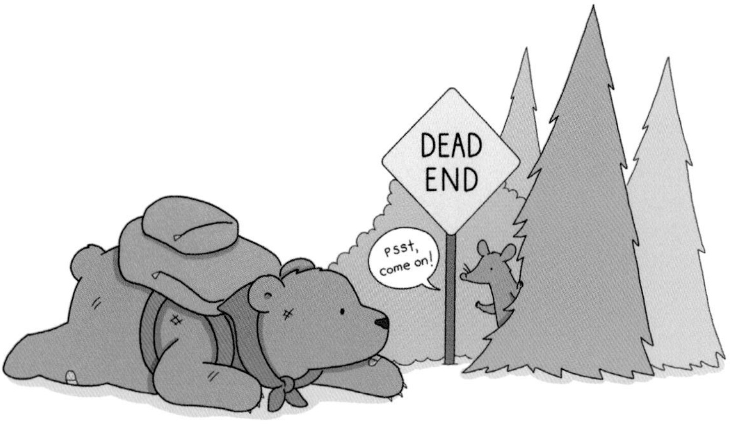
DEAD
END
psst, come on!

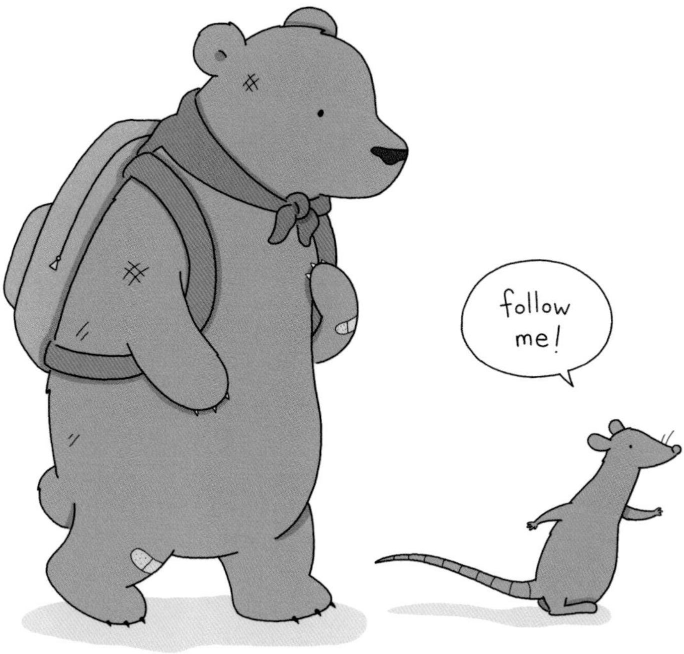
follow me!

when solace seems far,

never forget how amazing you are.

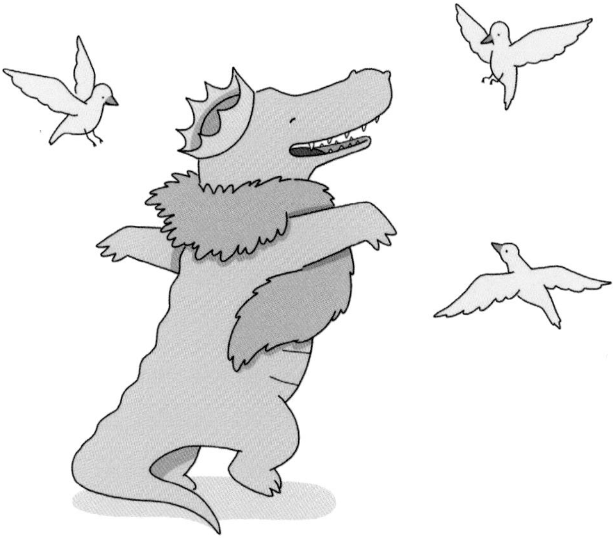

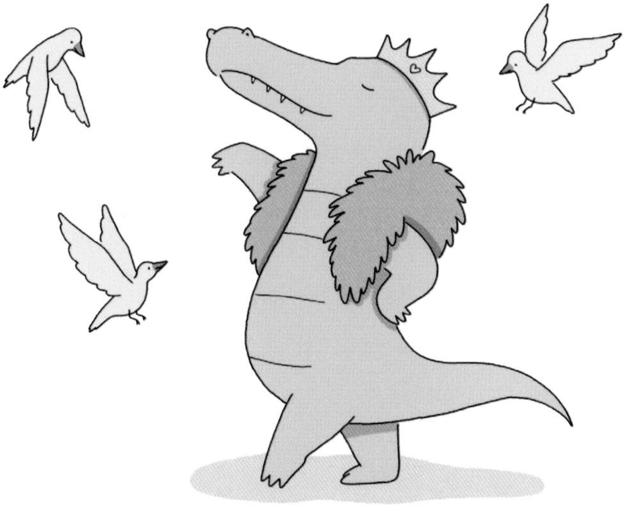

Just follow your heart

and you'll persevere.

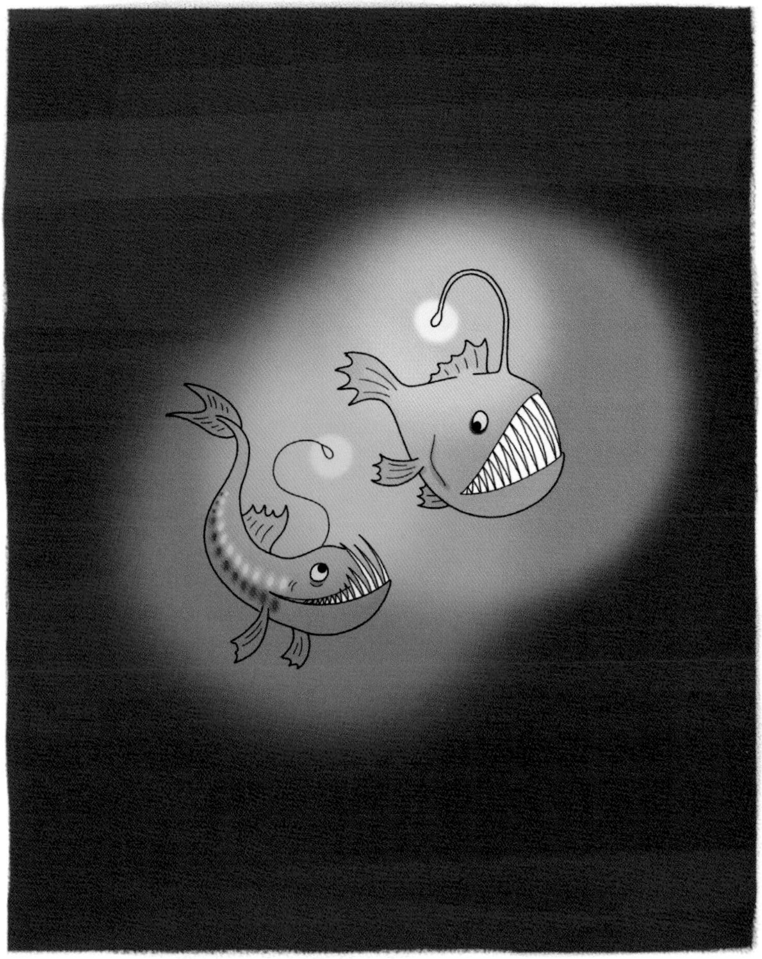

There's no one else like you

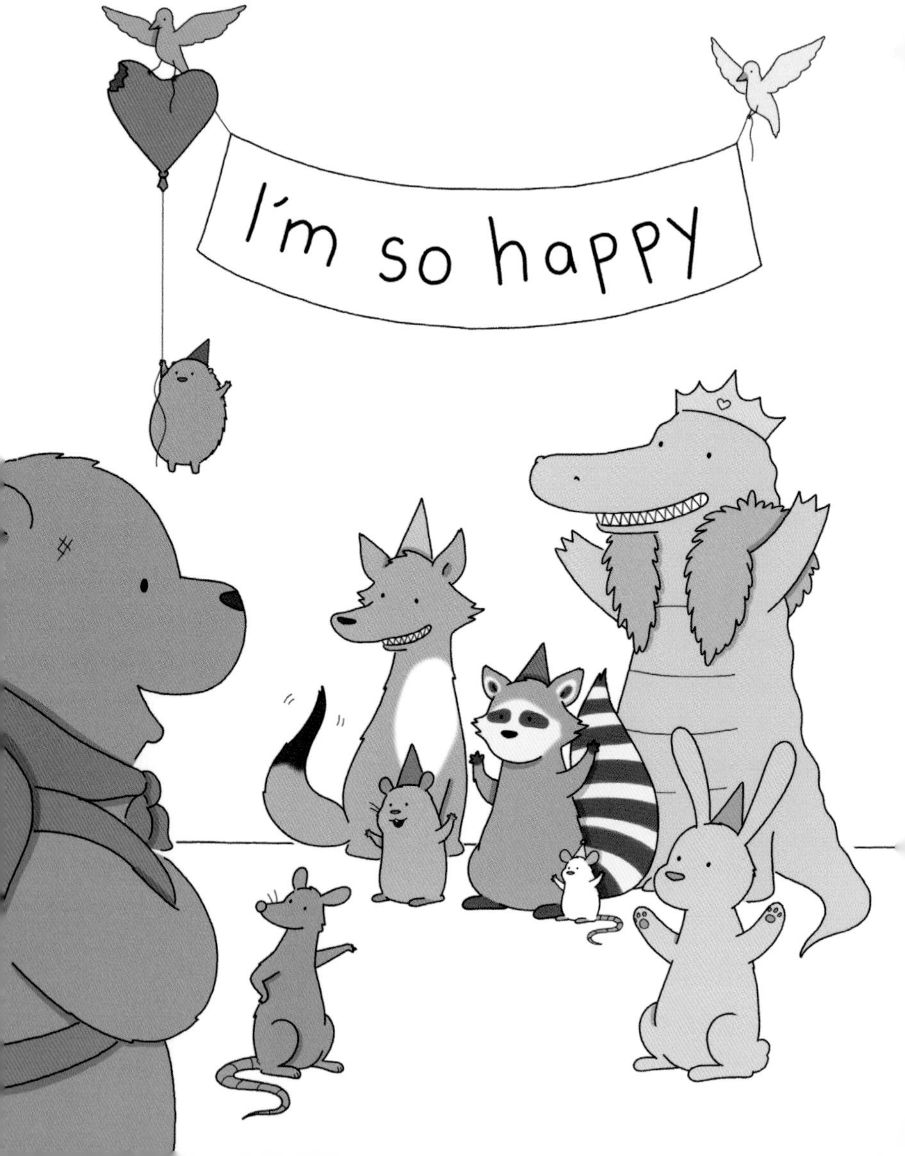
I'm so happy

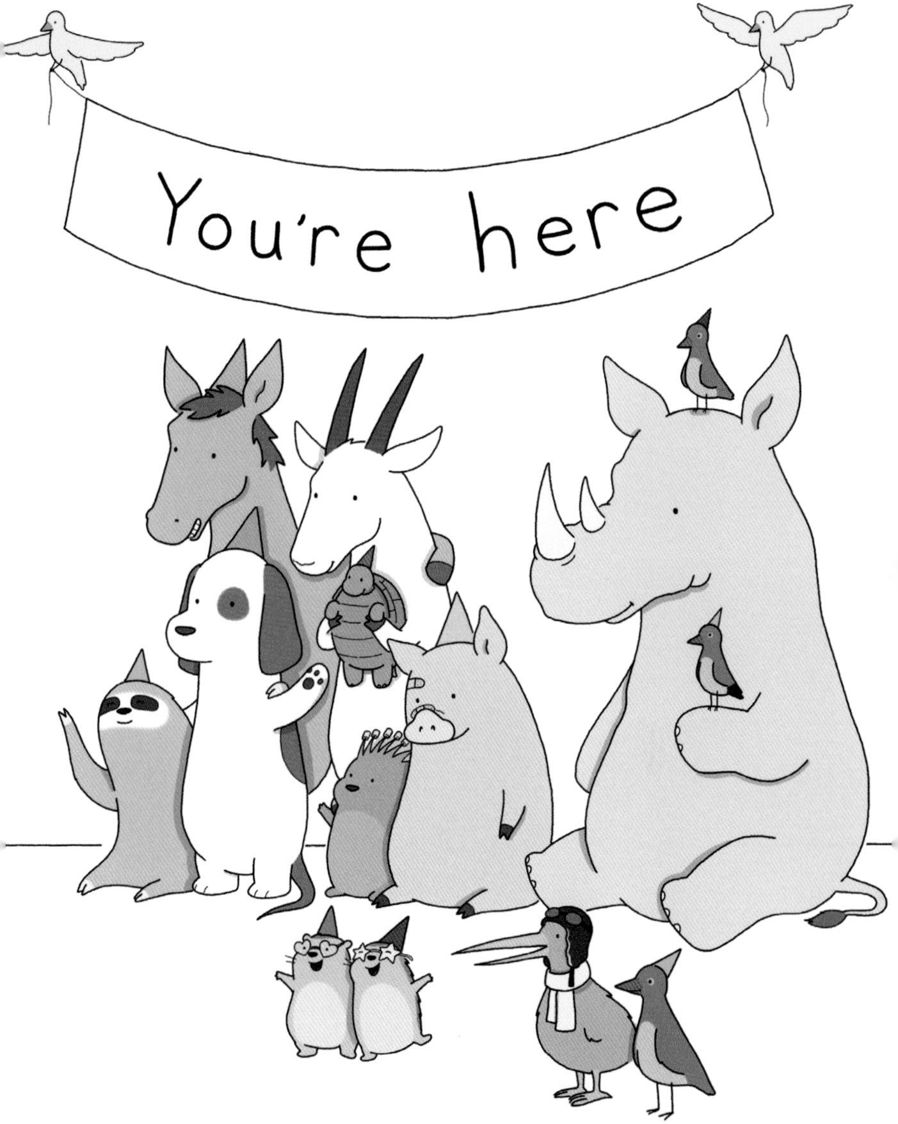
You're here

Acknowledgments

I would like to acknowledge and thank my incredible agent, Kathleen Ortiz, for all the hard work and guidance she has given me over the past several years. To my editor, Sydney Jeon, and to the entire team at Flatiron Books—it is always such a pleasure working with you. Thank you for believing in my vision for this book and helping me see it through. To my fabulous assistant, Julia, for helping me keep my head above water. To my family and dear friends, especially my wonderful husband and daughter, and my dad, brother, and sister—thank you for always supporting me no matter what. To my mom, who loved me so unconditionally she made it easy for me to love myself. Thank you to anyone who has ever taken the time to come to one of my book events, or written a kind note under one of my social media posts, or written to me directly, or just enjoyed my work quietly. I appreciate you so much. You are the reason I keep doing this. I'd like to acknowledge anyone reading this who is currently struggling or has ever struggled to feel accepted, understood, or loved. Remember to make room for the ones who see how you shine. I'm so happy you're here—this book is for you.

About the Author

LIZ CLIMO is a cartoonist, children's book author, illustrator, and animator. She grew up in the San Francisco Bay Area and moved to Los Angeles after college to work as a character artist on *The Simpsons*. She is the author of *You're Mom, You're Dad*, the Rory the Dinosaur series, *The Little World of Liz Climo, Lobster Is the Best Medicine*, and more! Her books have been translated into over a dozen languages and have sold millions of copies worldwide. She lives in Los Angeles with her husband and daughter.